STITCHERY

Free Expression

STITCHERY

Free Expression

FABRICS, STITCHES, DESIGNS

ANN WOELDERS

VNR VAN NOSTRAND REINHOLD COMPANY
NEW YORK   CINCINNATI   TORONTO   LONDON   MELBOURNE

Design and Photographs by C. Koevets, Santpoort

Library of Congress Catalog Card Number 72-7848
ISBN 0 442 29973 7

This book is set in Monophoto Bembo and is
printed in Great Britain by Jolly & Barber Ltd., Rugby,
and is bound by The Ferndale Book company.

Van Nostrand Reinhold Company Regional Offices:
New York Cincinnati Chicago Millbrae Dallas

Van Nostrand Reinhold Company International Offices:
London Toronto Melbourne

Published by Van Nostrand Reinhold Company, Inc.,
450 West 33rd Street, New York, N.Y. 10001 and
Van Nostrand Reinhold Company Ltd.,
25–28 Buckingham Gate, London SW1E 6LQ.

Published simultaneously in Canada by Van Nostrand
Reinhold Company Ltd.

16 15 14 13 12 11 10 9 8 7 6 5 4 3 2 1

CONTENTS

INTRODUCTION

It is very important that people should be able to express their creative impulses in their leisure-time activities. By developing the imagination you can find ways of expressing your own personality more clearly. You become more conscious of yourself, realising that you can create something through your own efforts, instead of simply copying the work of other people. Embroidery is one of the most pleasant of all leisure-time occupations. It can be done without set patterns, although a good design can help beginners to develop a sense of colour and basic technical skills.

Even those of you who are not all that good at drawing need not be put off by the idea of doing creative embroidery. Geometrical shapes offer a variety of subjects, from which you can choose your own. Anyone can draw them with the aid of compasses and a ruler. Practice with these simple shapes will lead to greater certainty of touch and the confidence to try less conventional shapes. After attempting a variety of forms you will soon notice that you can do more things than you thought. One person may be good at drawing stylized bird-shapes – a marvellous subject, capable of unlimited variations, another may be good at animals, and again the choice of shape and its applications is very wide. If you cannot draw, you should probably keep to circles, triangles and squares from which very satisfying compositions and patterns can be made.

However, the desire to make something yourself is not sufficient without the acquisition of a certain amount of technical skill. Anyone can do appliqué work – you do not need to know very many stitches, but the patterns become really interesting and pleasant to look at when a variety of stitches are used. For this reason, the book treats fabrics, stitches and designs together hoping to impress upon the reader the importance of the interaction between these elements.

The desire to try something new is the real motive force behind this form of spontaneous needlecraft. Apart from the enjoyment derived from the work itself, it is also a means of creating attractive and useful objects. This should encourage you to approach appliqué work and embroidery with care and thought as well as spontaneity.

Finally, let me wish you all a lot of fun with your creative needle-craft.   *A.W.*

WHAT YOU NEED

Needlework is a hobby which requires comparatively few tools: needles, scissors, pins, a thimble (which few people use), material and thread.

It is important, however, to have a wide selection of good needles of various types and sizes, including crewel needles (with points) and tapestry needles (without points). The chief things to remember are that the thread must pass easily through the eye of the needle and that it must be possible to pull both through the material without difficulty. Struggling with needles, thread and material which weren't meant for each other tends to be very discouraging. Pins must be sharp enough to slip easily through several layers of fabric at the same time, without leaving nasty holes in it. Glass-topped pins are especially useful in embroidery.

Usually one pair of scissors is not enough. For smaller pieces of material you will need a pair of small, pointed scissors, and, a medium-sized pair for heavier fabric. It is most important that scissors should be sharp or they will not be able to cut edges cleanly.

Always use good quality material and thread which will not fade in the sun or run when washed. It is not wise to economise on these when articles are intended to last for years.

As well as good material and sound tools, a minimum of technical skill is required. You should be able to control the needle properly, so that you can always be sure that it will come out in the right place. It does not matter whether this skill is acquired by doing cross-stitch or any other form of embroidery, as long as you can direct the needle correctly. If you do find that the needle is difficult to manage, it may be too long. Try using a shorter one – it will be easier.

MATERIAL

Appliqué is a technique by which a piece of material is decorated with patches of a different material. These patches should not be made of old pieces of fabric because they would soon show signs of wear and tear. The chief reason for using this technique is that it is a quick way of producing a design on the material. It is especially useful for decorating articles with a practical use – children's clothing, tea-cosies, cushions, oven-gloves and so on. The method is also used to obtain colour combinations and contrasts in texture which would not be possible with embroidery alone.

The choice of possible materials is vast – heavy, light, loosely or tightly woven, plain or patterned, matt or shiny, rough or smooth. There are so many different kinds of material that, at first it is quite difficult to choose the best.

Material must be chosen with its intended purpose in mind; it would be ludicrous to make a pair of oven-gloves out of lawn, which would be much too thin. It would be equally ridiculous to make them out of thick curtain material which could not be washed. Thin material would be unsuitable as the background in a wall hanging where a rough, strong material would look much better and be in keeping with the dimensions. The beginner should really keep to one kind of material – cotton for example. This offers a wide variety of choice and does not discolour or shrink.

After this first trial period, you can experiment with other materials, but a composition made exclusively from cotton fabrics often seems spoilt by the addition of a patch of silk or wool. These materials are rather dominant and catch the eye; wool often seems too rough and silk too shiny. However, if a particular area of a pattern has to be accentuated, then they too can be very effective. On the whole, it is risky to use different kinds of material, and the beginner should be cautious.

If when creating a design a lighter or fresher note is needed a livelier piece of material can be added. But if the design looks too restless because of the number of different kinds of materials, or because too many patterns are juxtaposed, it becomes more difficult to remedy.

You should choose the background material first. Colour and quality should be selected with the eventual use of the material in mind. As the choice of background is a conscious one it would be illogical to sew on so many patches that it is completely covered. But why choose a particular material for a background, and not just a cheap remnant?

The purpose of appliqué work, combined with free embroidery, is to make a harmonious whole out of the background fabric and the sewn-on patches. The background then plays a crucial part in achieving this total effect and is more than just a piece of material onto which the patches are sewn.

1

SAMPLES

If you take an arbitrary handful of samples of various fabrics out of the rag-bag, you will be struck by the differences in their texture. However, let us leave aside material with a printed pattern for the time being.

Tightly-woven, smooth materials (Nos. 1 and 2 in *fig. 1*) are especially suitable for appliqué work because they do not fray easily. The warp and the weft of the example shown in No. 1 are in different colours, giving the material a very lively appearance. In No. 2 the warp is not of uniform thickness and the material has a stripey effect. Samples 3, 4, 5 and 6 demonstrate clearly the importance of the thickness and regularity of the thread. Even the method of weaving creates differences in texture, as can be seen in samples 6, 7, and 8.

Loosely-woven materials offer very different possibilities, because the background material is always more or less visible through them. A layer of tulle, for example, can create the impression of changing colours, suggesting shapes rather than relying on sharply defined outlines. If you were to use a piece of one of these materials as part of the background material the finished article would be transparent. First, learn to *see* the differences between the various materials, then carefully explore and use their many possibilities.

1. A dip into the rag-bag. All plain materials, but still very varied.

2. See-through materials. The background remains visible through patches made of these fabrics.

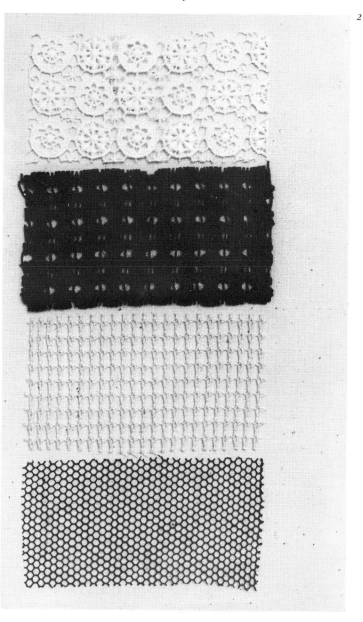

2

MATERIAL IS MADE UP OF THREAD

Material is more than just a surface of a certain colour and texture. It is composed of thick or thin threads, which can lie close together or far apart and these may be interwoven or knitted. That is why a piece of material can be changed in appearance when threads are pulled out, making a fringe. There are numerous ways of unravelling the threads of a piece of material and you can explore a lot of its characteristics by simply playing around in this way. The threads which have been drawn out can be used again, and they are obviously always of the right colour for the material. The undulating line which the weaving has given them makes them even more interesting to work with. *3*

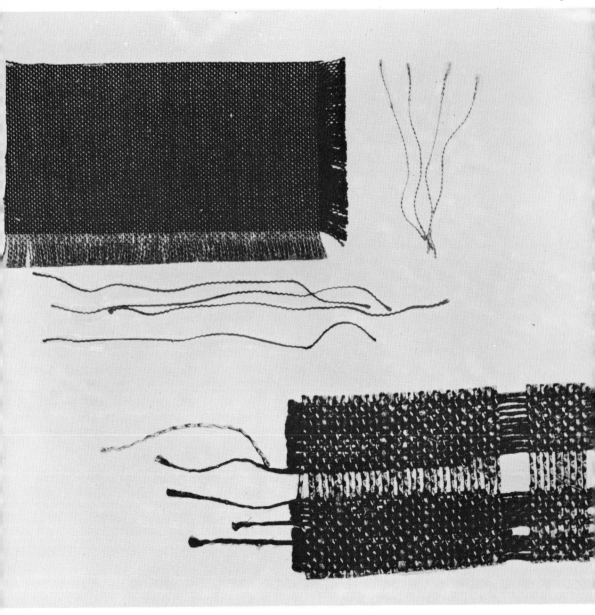

Sometimes totally unexpected qualities are to be found in a piece of material. Below, for example, a sample of a curtain material made out of cotton and linen is shown. This piece is not in fact woven, but crocheted or knitted, and by pulling at certain threads, it is possible to undo whole rows. In this way, strips can be made along which the stitches stand up and these can be arranged in arch shapes, or straight strips which look like ladders with crossed rungs. It is only when you start cutting, pulling threads out, folding the material and generally playing about with it that these qualities become apparent.

3. *Material can be changed by pulling the threads out. These threads can be used again very easily.*

4. *Unravelling sometimes produces surprising results.*

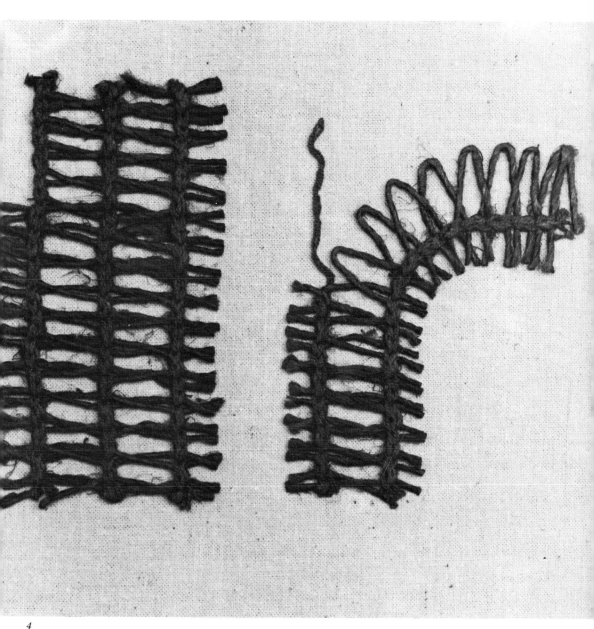

4

THREAD

5. Thick and thin, rough and smooth – various kinds of threads.

6. Threads have all sorts of possibilities: splitting, unwinding, forming loops or bundles, or coiling up when one of the strands is pulled out.

5

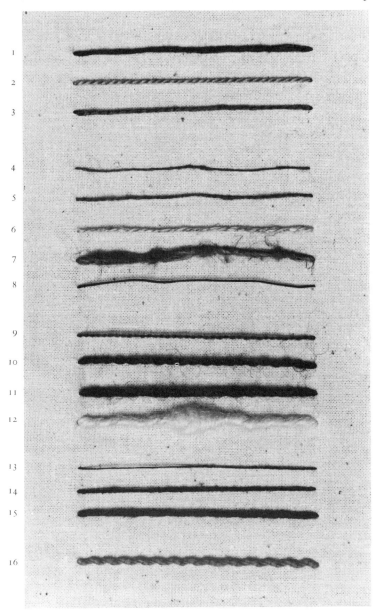

After considering the material *on* which we embroider and sew, we must look at the material *with* which we embroider and sew. There are innumerable kinds of threads and yarns and with new ones always appearing on the market it is impossible to talk about all of them here.

In addition to the traditional ones – wool, linen, silk and cotton – there are a large number of synthetic threads and yarns: for example, synthetic knitting yarn, nylon, plastic, gold and silver lurex thread. Look around the shops to see which kinds are available and gradually try to build up a reserve in a variety of colours and shades. Don't forget to look in shops which specialise in ropes and fishing equipment. Some people prefer to work with rough thread rather than thin yarn. The following kinds of thread will be well known to you: stranded cotton, pearl cotton, linen yarn and silk. Each one has its own special characteristics and qualities, some are smooth and shiny, others rough and dull; some can be divided, while others are made out of a single strand.

Here are examples of several kinds of thread. First we have three smooth types:

1. Stranded cotton.
2. Pearl cotton (Sylko perlé).
3. Silk.

Then we have five kinds of linen thread:

4. One-ply linen thread.
5 and 6. Two-ply linen thread.
7. Irregular loosely-spun linen thread.
8. A variety of fishing line.

Here are four kinds which are dull and woolly:

9 and 10. Worsted.

11. Four-ply wool.

12. Irregularly spun wool.

And finally the dull cotton yarns:

13. Thin embroidery cotton.

14. A thicker embroidery cotton.

15. D.M.C. or Clark's soft embroidery cotton.

16. Rubbed yarn.

These varieties of yarn cannot all be used indiscriminately. Some are especially suitable for embroidery, others are better used for couching either as single threads or in bunches. But there is more to thread than those straight lengths shown in the photograph. It can be bent in all directions, it can be twisted, knotted or interwoven. For instance, try splitting a length of thread by twisting the ends in opposite directions. Unravelling it can prove very interesting. Try dropping a length of thread on a piece of material and see what shapes it takes. Place a bunch of the same thread on the same material and see how that looks. If you are using two or more ply thread, made out of twisted strands, you can pull at one of the strands and watch the results – a strange-looking length of thread with a lot of tiny loops. And all from what was an ordinary piece of thread!

It is important to use your imagination in getting to know every kind of thread and its properties. See, for example, how stranded cotton can be split and be made to assume all sorts of shapes, instead of being a simple, dead length of yarn. Irregularly spun linen thread will become soft and fluffy when the ends are twisted in opposite directions and even looks lighter in colour in some places.

All this becomes clear when you start working and experimenting. Only frequent practice and experience will teach us the possibilities – and limitations – of thread.

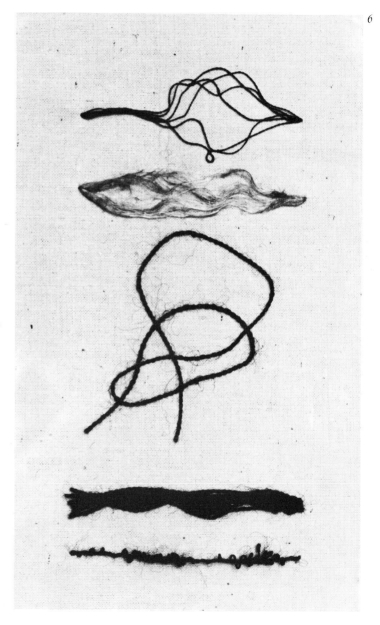

6

13

7. The patches are cut in such a way that the direction of the thread coincides with that in the background material.

8. Only when the design of the patches is more important than the direction of the thread can they be sewn on against the run of the thread in the background material.

9. The pattern, on which the direction of the thread is indicated, is pinned on a piece of material. Whether the patch is cut with or without allowance for a hem depends on how it is going to be applied (see pages 16 and 17).

CUTTING AND APPLYING THE FABRIC SHAPES

One of the most important conditions for successful appliqué work is that the shapes to be sewn on should be simple ones. Firstly it is not as easy to cut shapes out of material as it is out of paper. Material has a very different texture, and tends to fray if cut into sharp points or thin strips. A complicated shape is also difficult to sew on and often gives an impression of untidiness.

The parts which are to be attached should be cut in such a way that the threads run in the same direction as those in the background material (see *fig. 7*). This rule should only be departed from when the design depends on it (see *fig. 8*). The pattern of flower leaves has been cut to resemble organic cells and it was not possible to cut the leaves so that the threads would run in the right way. In this case the pattern was the most important element to be considered.

The direction of threads is worked out on the patterns for appliqué, which are first cut out in paper. Next the pattern is pinned on the background material, with or without allowance being made for the seam, depending on the way the patch will be put on. (See *page 17* on sewing.)

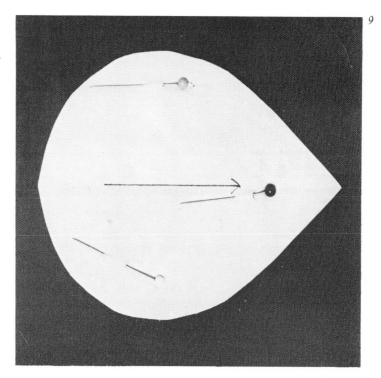

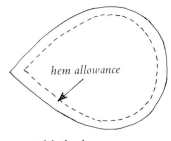

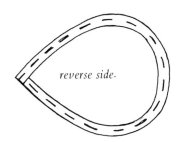

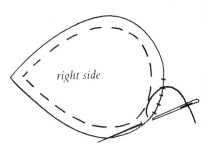

10. 1st Method
(i) *Cut patch with a small extra allowance for the hem.*

(ii) *Turn hem under and tack (baste).*

(iii) *Sew patch on to background with invisible stitches.*

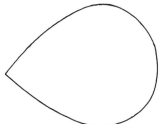

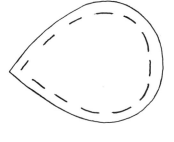

11. 2nd Method
(i) *Cut patch without extra allowance for hem.*

(ii) *Tack (baste) patch on background material.*

(iii) *Sew patch on with button-hole stitches.*

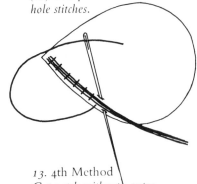

12. 3rd Method
Cut patch without extra allowance for hem and tack (baste) to background as in fig. 11, i and ii, then sew it on with darning stitches.

13. 4th Method
Cut patch without extra allowance for hem, then tack (baste) it to background, as in fig. 11, (i) and (ii), then sew it on with couching stitches. The thread must be close to the edge of the patch and the overcast stitches should not be too far apart.

16

SEWING

Patches can be sewn together and applied in various ways. In our illustrations (*figs. 10, 11, 12 and 13*) a simple leaf-shape is shown, but it could have been any shape. There are four basic ways of sewing, though, with a little imagination, it would be possible to think of many more.

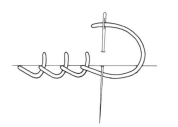

14. Buttonhole stitch.

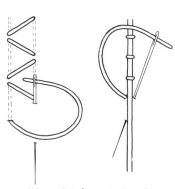

15. Wave Stitch. 16. Couching.

APPLIQUE METHODS – USING THE BACKGROUND MATERIAL

The four methods just mentioned are those most often used to sew on patches. They all have advantages and disadvantages and the choice of a particular method depends on the effect desired.

Method 1 is the most common in some countries, but sometimes folding the seam is not very easy and the greatest disadvantage is that the seam can look lumpy underneath. There is a tendency for the turning to pucker, especially on curves, unless it is snipped carefully. This method also makes the patch stand out very sharply against the background, unless the transition is made less abrupt with couching or a row of running stitches, as in *fig. 20*. The main advantage of this method is that the patches are secure, the fabric does not fray and the finished article can be washed very easily.

Method 2 has the advantage that the shape of the pattern can be cut without making an extra allowance for the seam. This method allows the patch to be sewn on firmly, but it is sometimes difficult to get the loops of the stitches completely regular – a freer, irregular effect may, however, be preferred. The stitches stand out very clearly between the patch and the background material, making a sharp contour which is often difficult to tone down.

Methods 3 and 4, using wave stitches and couching, are both very good. It is a great advantage to be able to cut out the shapes without making other allowances, and, when the patches are sewn on with small stitches, the finished work will be strong enough to stand up to thorough washing. In the case of the wave stitch you can use a single thread of thin embroidery cotton; for the couching you can use a full stranded cotton (*six-ply*), which can be sewn down with a single thread of the same or a contrasting colour.

These last two methods make it much easier to blend the patch into the background, thus making the finished pattern a more satisfying unity.

In *fig. 20* you can see four patches sewn on, each according to one of the four different methods. On the outer edges of the patches you can see the sort of outline produced when the different methods are followed; the inner edges show how the patches are attached by the stitches and thread to the background material to form the finished work.

The transition from the patches to the background material can be made in the following ways:

Above left: method 1
A row of running stitches is embroidered in light thread along the edge of the darker material, and just round the edge of the patch there is another row in dark thread.

Above right: method 2
Along the edge outside the darker patch is a row of buttonhole stitches.

Below left: method 3
The darker shape of the patch has been extended by an extra row of wave stitches, reinforced with chain stitches or French knots.

Below right: method 4
The outline is changed by sewing the patch down with darker thread.

18. Fly Stitch.

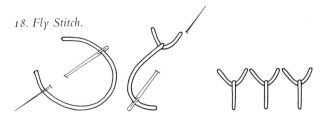

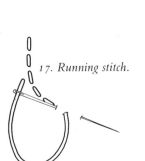

17. Running stitch.

19. French knots.

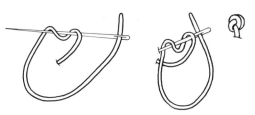

20. Four ways of fastening the patches on. The transition from the patch to the background material is made to appear gradual.

It can be seen that dark thread used round a dark patch makes the patch look bigger than it really is. If you want to make it look smaller – by drawing the colour of the background material into the patch – then you should use a light-coloured thread on a dark patch.

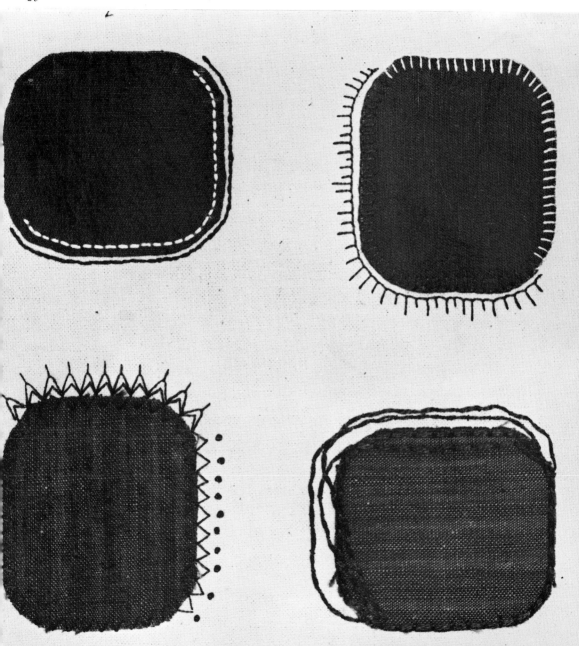

GEOMETRICAL SHAPES

RECTANGLE

Everybody can draw a rectangle, a circle, a heart shape, or a simple leaf shape. A lot of interesting and very personal pieces of work can be based on these simple shapes. They can be used as the basic patterns for appliqué work on articles intended for practical use, but are also perfectly suitable for wall hangings and other decorative articles.

The simplest shape is probably the rectangle, which can vary in form from a square to a long strip. Try cutting out rectangles of various shapes and sizes from paper – colourful pages from a woman's magazine, perhaps, or wrapping paper, or pieces of wallpaper. Choose matching colours and make a composition from them in say yellow. Don't forget to add orange-coloured bits as well as greenish ones. You can also choose papers which are more or less of similar colour, but of different texture. Try, for example, a combination of brown wrapping paper, thin brown cardboard or corrugated cardboard, smooth or ribbed paper from a chocolate box, gold paper, and so on.

Once the rectangles have been cut out, they should be placed on a sheet of smooth paper. They can then be shifted about and arranged into a pattern in which they partly cover one another. It is also important to pay attention to the spaces which are left between the shapes, since they also play their part. A nicely balanced composition, can be made in this way quite easily, but it is essential to keep the lines running horizontally and vertically. The rectangular shapes should not be placed slanting or askew.

Try this method for making a border, or filling up a particular surface with a similar composition. The rectangles can be placed as strips, with all the long sides running in the same direction. The monotony of this arrangement can then be broken by placing one of the rectangles so that it runs in the other direction. This will make the composition more lively. Introducing a circle or semi-circle helps considerably to soften the strict lines of the rectangles and adds interest to the whole design.

After carrying out these preliminary exercises in paper – it's cheaper than material – you can start on a piece of fabric. You can begin with a simple piece of material, but it is much more fun to begin by decorating some specific article, perhaps the edge of an apron, the border of a table mat or a cushion.

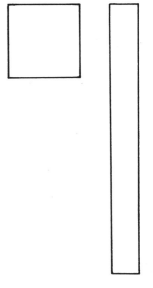

21. A square and a strip – both rectangles.

22. Rectangles can be used to make up a border. The border at the top is made up of materials of the same colour, but of different texture. At the bottom, various patterned materials have been used, but the colours are related: yellow, brown and a touch of violet.

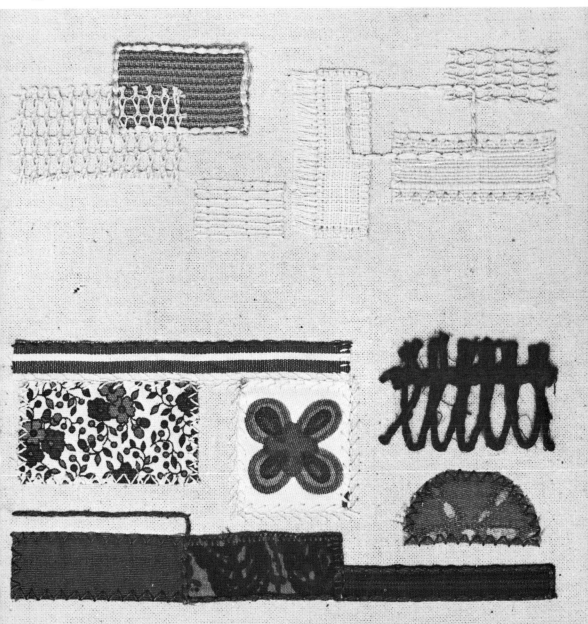

23

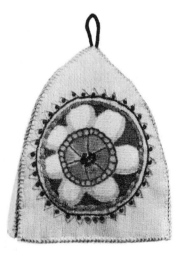

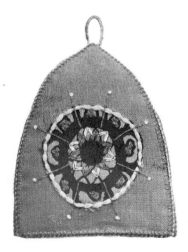

CIRCLE

A circle is a very pleasant shape to work with. If you are lucky enough to find material with circles already printed on it, this will provide a very suitable starting-point for your experiments. But first you must choose thread and material which will go with your printed circles.

Try cutting out several circles and sewing them on a background of the same colour, as has been done with the egg-cosies in *fig. 23* (see *page 90* about the finishing). Or cut out 3 to 5 similar circles and apply them in different ways on the same background, see *fig. 24*. One shape can be sewn on with a couching stitch and another with a wave stitch. The outline of the patch can be left sharp or made to blend with the background. Sometimes it is possible to make a light colour more eye-catching and, at others, to accentuate a dark one. The circles can be cut in half and the pattern of the patch can be continued in a further semicircle with embroidery. Or the middle of the circle can be cut out, then the inner circle and the outer ring can each be applied separately.

Fig. 24 shows four circular patches. The first one has a sharp outline, because the dark thread makes the dark colour of the patch stand out even more. The second patch blends progressively into the background. Much lighter coloured thread has been used and the dark material of the patch is almost covered by the embroidery stitches. The centre has been cut out of the third circle and the remaining ring has been sewn on with fly stitches which are continued on to the background material, giving the patch the appearance of a rayed sun (see *fig. 18* showing fly stitches). The fourth patch is in fact the middle of the third circle and the outer edge here is brought out by a couching stitch. These early experiments may occasionally seem tedious, but they can be quite amusing and are certainly very instructive, teaching the beginner to discover the possibilities of material.

23. *Round shapes of various materials have been used for the patches on these three egg-cosies.*

24. *Four circular shapes made from three circles. The shapes can be modified a lot, using various embroidery stitches.*

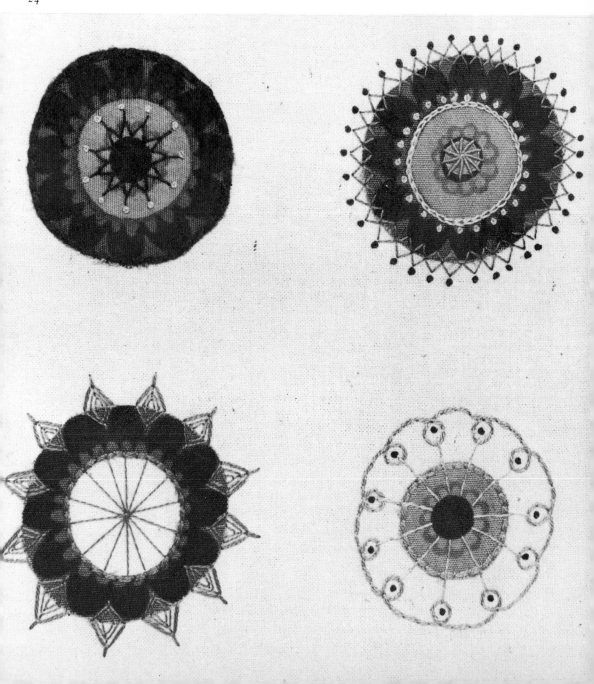

TRIANGLE

In spite of its simplicity, the triangle is a shape which can be used in a great number of combinations. Indeed, it is probably easier to make a composition with triangles than with circles. The circle is a closed shape, while the triangle – and, for that matter, the square, the pentagon and so on – can be built up in all directions, having common sides with other straight-sided shapes.

Triangles can be used alone as patches, or they can touch at one point; they can coincide along one side, or partly overlap. They can be used for borders, the central surfaces of articles or as parts of patterns combining with other shapes.

The star in *fig. 27* is composed of triangles which each have a common side with the pentagon in the centre. A check pattern was chosen for the point of the star and the background in the upper left corner. The dark checks form the point of the star and the light checks form the background. Notice the repeated motifs in this example of appliqué work:

1. the circular shape in the centre, the circle in the section above right, and the circle in the embroidered area;
2. the vertical lines of the check patch taken up in the two other background areas on the left;
3. and below right, where the light background runs over into the dark point of the star, and the dark colour seems to run out into the background on the other side.

25

26

25. *An equilateral triangle – a triangle with equal sides – is the basic shape in this border.*

26. *Irregular triangles placed next to each other, with one side along the edge. In spite of this irregularity, the border still gives a general impression of order.*

27. *A pentagonal star made up of triangles with a pentagon in the centre. Notice the recurrence of certain colours and shapes in this design. (see page 80, colour).*

27

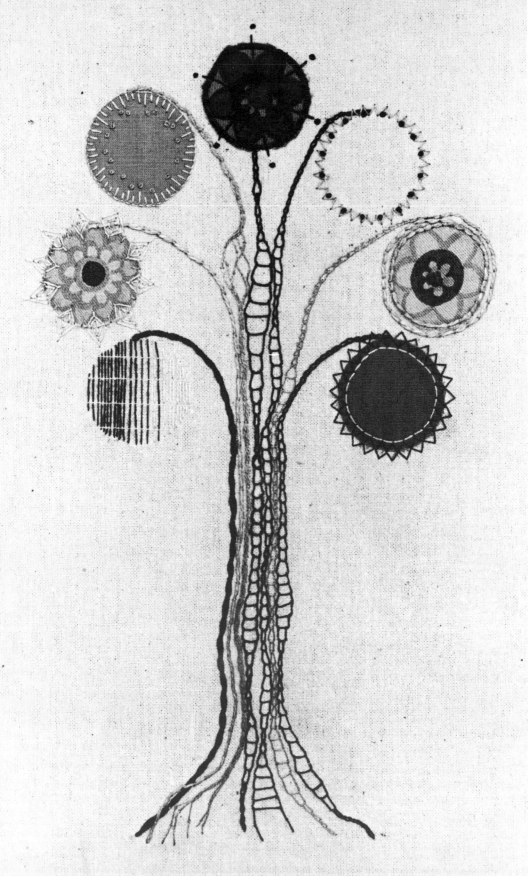

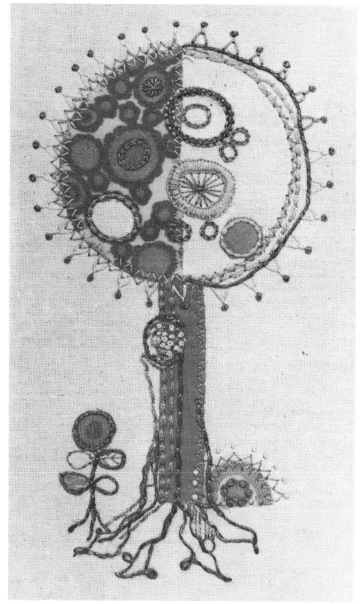

28. *A tree made with circles. Each leaf is attached to a branch. The branches come together to form the trunk, which splits into roots at the foot.*

29. *A tree full of oranges. Only half of the top part is an appliqué patch; an orange has been cut out and sewn on the other half. Similar shapes have been applied at the foot of the tree.*

29

COMPOSITE SHAPES

Geometrical shapes can be used in many ways, either alone or as parts of composite shapes. They can be the starting point for abstract decorative shapes or the basis of stylized natural forms, which do not need to be very complicated (see, for example, the tree-shape in *fig. 28*, in which the basic shape is a circle). By very simple means, the impression has been created of a tree standing straight and firm in the earth.

Half of the round top of the tree (*fig. 29*) is a sewn-on patch, while the other half is made up by embroidery which is a continuation of the pattern on the patch. At the foot of the tree are a number of round shapes cut from the printed material, which have been made to look like flowers, and another shape which resembles a sun. Cotton embroidery thread was used to couch a linen thread, the ends of which were split at the roots.

Other examples of trees, made from circles and strip shapes, can be seen on the back of the jacket and in *fig. 130* on *page 89*.

30. The basis of this design is four stripes of the same length and width, but each of a different colour: red, blue-green (the colour of the background material), yellow and orange. Circles and triangles have been cut out and sewn on at a little distance from the holes they have left. This design suggests a townscape, or rockets among heavenly bodies (see page 81, colour).

COMPOSITE AND STYLIZED SHAPES

More complicated stylized shapes can be built up from geometrical forms, too. There are plenty of subjects – cats, houses, flowers, sailing boats, to name only a few. Let us look at the example of a bird form here. The bird in *fig. 31* has been built up from geometrical shapes. In *fig. 32* the bird has been cut out of a single piece of material and its outline has been softened. Also look at the example of a bird shape on the cover of this book.

When you cut a shape out of a piece of printed material, you should look for anything in the actual pattern which could be of use in its application to the background material. In *fig. 32*, a light spot has been used to represent the bird's eye. Other spots emphasize the shape of the wing, and a few more have been embroidered in dark thread to mark the tail. It often needs a lot of patience to work out how a piece of material can best be used, but first of all you have to develop a good eye for combining the material and forms with which you are going to work.

The bird in *fig. 32* is only one example; other kinds of birds can be made with other material. The sketch in *fig. 31* can also be modified. If the neck, tail and legs were made longer, it would become a sort of imaginary bird as in *fig. 33*. If the tail and legs are omitted, it looks as though the bird is brooding or swimming.

The bird in *fig. 32* is made up of two concentric circles. If the head and tail are bent towards each other the bird looks almost spherical, as though sleeping or cleaning its feathers. Any new idea combined with a simple sketch, can be a starting-point (*fig. 34*).

31

31. Stylized bird with circles, triangles and rectangles as the basic shapes.

32. The outline is less sharp here and the bird is cut out of one piece of material. The eye is indicated by a spot, and more embroidered spots mark the wing.

33. The bird drawn in fig. 31 has been elongated to make a decorative imaginary bird.

33

32

FROM SKETCH
TO
EMBROIDERY

First a wing is added to the bird in *fig. 34*, then the body is made slightly fatter. The sketch is now ready for putting on. The bird-shape is cut out and divided into the following parts: tail, wing, head and body.

These parts are arranged in the correct place on the background material and a line of cotton is tacked (basted) round the outlines of these paper patterns, drawing the shape onto the background. It is better not to use pencil or chalk, since the marks might not come off completely later. Besides, even if the pencil mark itself has been obliterated, it tends to make the material a bit messy. Thread can always be taken out and used somewhere else, so your guide-lines can be easily removed. Next you must choose the material for the appliqué and the parts are cut out: the head, tail, part of the body and a circle for the wing. For the moment, they don't look quite the same as the parts of the paper pattern.

But as soon as a little thread is arranged in coils on the wing, the design looks more bird-like and ideas begin to flow. The thread on the wings is temporarily fastened in place with pins which are pushed through from the back of the material, so that they will not be in the way when the patches and thread have to be applied. When the patches are fastened on the material you can start the actual embroidery, and ideas will develop from this. Most of the embroidery work on this little bird pattern is in couching (see *fig. 16, page 17,* and also *pages 44–45).*

34
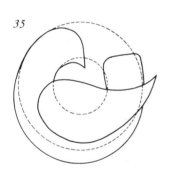

35
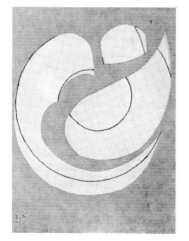

34. Even two concentric circles can make up a bird.

35. The drawing prepared.

36. The bird is cut out in the following parts: a wing, the tail and the head.

37. The drawing is transferred to the material by tacking (basting) round the paper pattern.

38. Once the material is chosen, the patches are cut out ready for application. Some surfaces can be elaborated with thread.

39. The bird is ready – ice-blue with a yellow-green wing (see page 82, colour.)

36
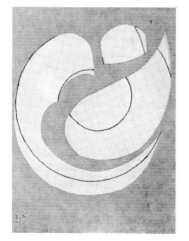

37
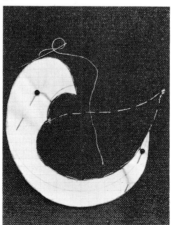

38
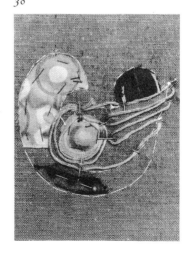

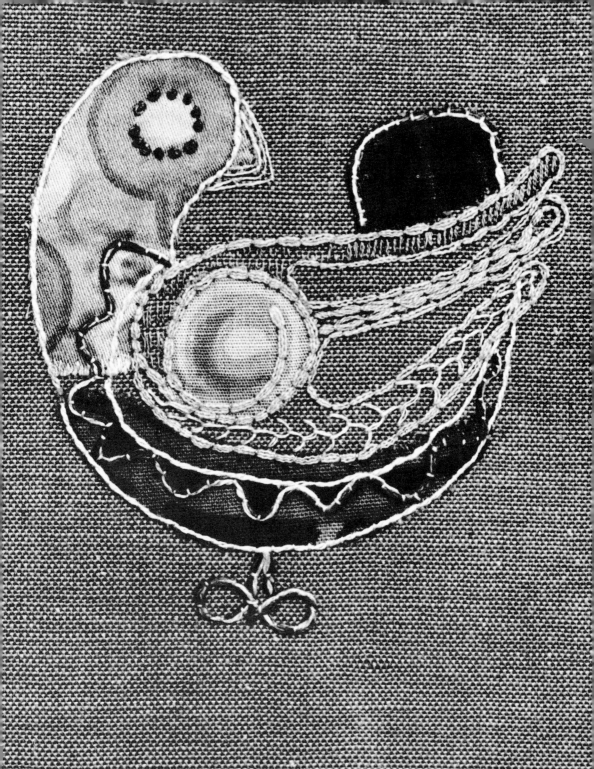

POSITIVE AND NEGATIVE SHAPES

40. *A positive shape is cut out and leaves behind a negative one.*

41. *Two different squares along the border of the material, where a triangle has been cut out. Above, the triangle has been turned over so that the reverse side is uppermost. Below, a triangle which has been turned 180°.*

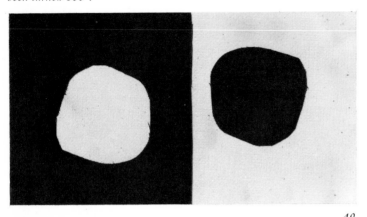

40

41

In the examples which I have discussed up to this point, I have confined myself to positive shapes, that is, shapes which have actually been cut out of material.

When a shape is cut out of a piece of material we are left with a hole in the fabric. This space has the same shape as the piece which has just been cut out. It is called a negative shape and is defined by the material around it (*fig. 40*). To achieve real interaction between the applied pieces and the background material both positive and negative pieces should be used. The positive shapes add new colours and textures to the background, while the negative shapes allow the background to be integrated into the total composition.

Brand new possibilities are opened up when a shape is cut out along the edge of a piece of fabric and then placed next to the space it has left in the material. A completely new shape comes to life, formed by juxtaposing a positive and negative shape. A semicircle cut out along the edge of a piece of material, forms a full circle when placed alongside the space left by it. Similarly, a right angle triangle with two equal sides and with its third side along the edge of the material will form a square with a perpendicular diagonal. If a triangle with unequal sides is cut out, turned *180°* in the same plane and placed alongside the space it has left a parallelogram is produced (see *fig. 41*).

Many fabrics are different according to which side you look at them, having a lighter and a darker side (fig. 42). With this type of material, the interaction of positive and negative shapes can be used along the hem (see fig. 43). The material in this example is darker on the upper side and lighter underneath. The hem has been turned towards the upper side and the cut-out triangles taken from the hem are placed with the reverse of the material upwards, against the space from which they have been cut. The two added lines of thread give an impression of undulating movement, giving rhythm and life to what is otherwise a very simple pattern. When both sides of the material are used for a hem in this way the cut-out shapes must be turned 180° in the same plane and put opposite the spaces they have left, if simply turned over they would not be visible. The material should be pleasing or interesting in some way on both sides. If the pattern on the reverse looks hazy or ill-defined, it will not usually provide a sufficient contrast. Materials like denim, which have a darker and lighter side resulting from the weaving process, are ideal for this kind of work. They can be used to make aprons with a border round the hem, Fig. 44 shows a design for a border in this style. These very simple shapes are particularly agreeable to work with and a little imagination can produce good results.

42. Denim, with its lighter and darker sides.

43. Three small triangles applied next to the spaces. The linen threads embroidered over it tend to soften the outline and bring rhythm and movement to the composition.

44. Design for a border or decorative strip separating light and dark material.

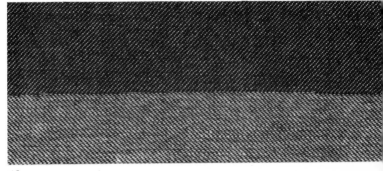

42

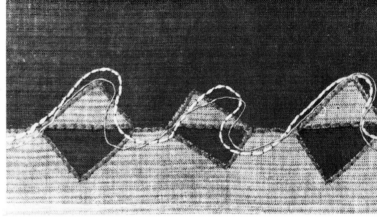

43

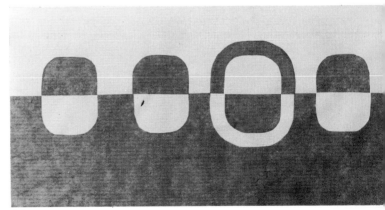

44

The use of positive and negative shapes will help to create a sense of harmony between two kinds of material; it will also make the transition from one kind of material to another easier or even help to create a composition in which the interest lies in having dark and light areas.

Study the examples on these pages carefully, they show how you can experiment with cutout shapes.

45. Geometrical figures in a composition with a lighter and darker side.

46. The weather house; she is positive, he negative, but both make attractive designs (see page 83, colour).

The shapes we are about to discuss are very similar to the geometrical forms and are just as much fun to work with. We will take for our examples heart shapes and leaf shapes.

The heart should be cut out symmetrically, as should the leaf. That is why it is first necessary to make a paper pattern. The piece of paper is folded in two and the shape is cut out from the fold, so that the two halves of the form will be exactly equal.

SIMPLE SHAPES

HEART SHAPES

47. Shapes and colours should be repeated in a composition – here both the heart and the circle. The same applies to the material.

48. Positive and negative shapes have been used in this composition. The smallest heart has been cut out of the centre; the large heart is partly appliqué, partly embroidery.

Heart shapes can be used for borders as well as for whole compositions. They can be combined with other shapes, as can be seen on the oven-gloves and the leaf design on *page 39*. The heart composition on *page 37*, shows clearly how positive and negative shapes can both play an important part. The smallest heart has been cut from the centre of the material and then sewn on above; the largest heart is a negative shape, surrounded by a number of decorative areas, some which have been applied and some of which are simply embroidered.

LEAF SHAPES

A leaf can be as long and narrow as a crocus leaf, or as wide as that of a sunflower. The edges can be deeply split and jagged, or quite unbroken. Sometimes a leaf pattern is made up of a number of smaller leaves. Sometimes it has a long stalk, sometimes a short one, or none at all. Perhaps it has a smaller leaf attached to it.

There are quite a lot of details to take into account and plenty of shapes from which to choose. Do be sure to look in which direction the veins run, because this can be very different according to the kind of leaf. The individual characteristics of leaves can be the basis for inventiveness and variation in stitching and in the applied pieces.

In any case, the object is not to imitate nature, or to make an exact copy of it. An abstract leaf shape is more worthwhile than an imitation which can never equal nature itself in wonder and beauty.

But do notice a few details, choose some of them and concentrate on these in the application. They should be exaggerated, but the shapes themselves should be kept as simple as possible.

The three leaves in *fig. 50* form a detail of a small wall hanging. The shape of each leaf is the same, but the size varies. Indeed, the leaves of a plant are usually smaller the higher up the plant they are. A small heart shape has been cut out of the middle leaf and applied to the smallest one.

49. Simple leaf shapes, positive and negative.

50. Three leaves from a wall hanging. Similar in shape, but different in size, because leaves often become smaller in size higher up the plant.

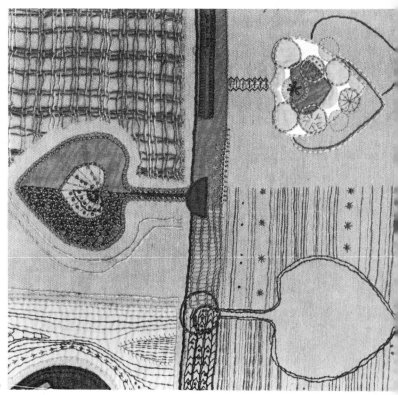

50

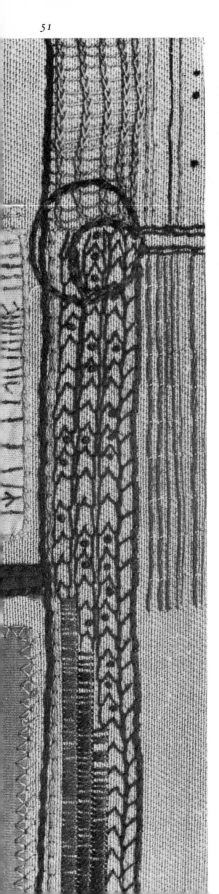

EMBROIDERED SURFACES

In the case of the heart shape on *page 37* and the leaf shape on *page 39*, you can see how a surface can be created with stitchery. If thread of the same colour as the background material is used for the embroidery, there will be a change simply in the texture of the background. Using thread of a different colour from the background means that lighter or darker areas can be created. This effect can be used to make patterns such as stripes, lines, ribs, cells or graining, and there are many more variations which it is impossible to describe by any particular name. All these patterned surfaces do have something in common, their effect cannot be achieved just with appliqué.

If you are very fond of embroidery, it is sometimes difficult to restrain yourself from trying new variations on standard stitches. It is easy to forget too that the undecorated areas, in which the background material can be seen to full advantage also play a part in a composition. The stitches you can use are: darning, various kinds of chain stitch, four-sided stitch, French knots and couching.

On the following pages we will deal with these types of stitch. You will find numerous different kinds suggested in our examples, though new ones can always be found by experimenting. The examples are intended to inspire the reader to extend her own range of stitches. Some of the stitches look very simple, but if put on irregularly or very close together, they can create textures and surfaces which are full of life. Books on stitches are another very good source of new ideas.

It is not, in fact, necessary to know very many stitches, as long as you understand how to vary what you do know. You can change them by making them smaller or bigger, or by giving them an irregular shape, by embroidering them on top of one of another, or by using different kinds of thread. The use of several kinds of thread, as well as different kinds of stitches, might produce an untidy effect though, so don't forget this basic rule of thumb: one kind of stitch with different kinds of thread, or, various kinds of stitches with the same kind of thread.

51. *Detail of the trunk, in which lots of different stitches have been used.*

52. *Waves – a wonderful subject. This wave has been frozen in its movement and finally become a circle. The effect of stiffness is accentuated by darning.*

53. *There is more life in these waves, where the water actually seems to be moving. Couching gives more freedom to the lines.*

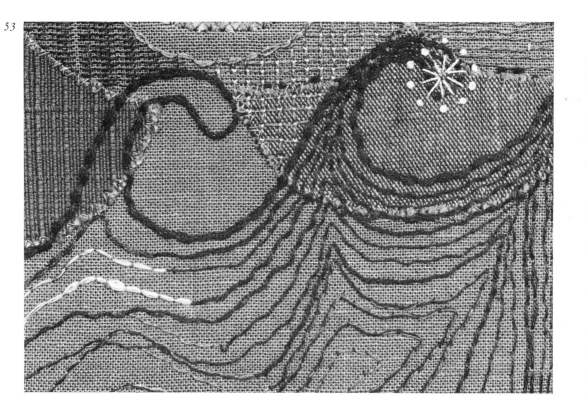

DARNING

The simplest stitch is probably darning stitch. Even children can make patterns and fill surfaces with these up-and-down stitches. It is possible to create the effect of woven thread by doing rows of darning stitch. If you have done a lot of cross-stitch and drawn or pulled fabric work, you will find it very difficult to start stitching and embroidering irregularly. After aiming at perfect regularity, it is hard to forget this and embroider freely.

In a very tightly-woven material the stitches tend to become irregular automatically as it is impossible to count the threads. In many of the illustrations, including those showing the varieties of stitches, the material used is colourfast cotton, which is often very pretty to look at and pleasant to work on. It does have one disadvantage, it shrinks when washed.

In *fig. 57,* darning stitches have been used to cover a whole surface. On the left of the photograph, the stitches have been embroidered with different threads at irregular intervals. In the centre, thread of the same colour as the background material has been used. The stitches have been made progressively smaller in two places, so that the horizontal lines bulge slightly. Here and there a knot has been made in the yarn, which makes a lively variation.

Further on, less and less fabric is left between the stitches, until only one thread is picked up by the needle. Darker colours are used, the direction of the stitches is altered, and a whole network of lines develops which looks something like the texture of the trunk of a tree.

Finally, in the smaller area on the right, a whole series of darning stitches have been arbitrarily embroidered through each other.

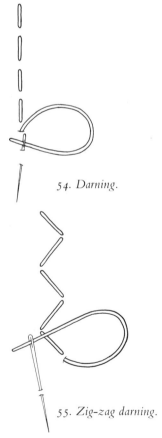

54. *Darning.*

55. *Zig-zag darning.*

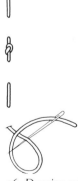

56. *Darning with a knot in the thread.*

57

The next stitch we are going to discuss is not, strictly speaking, a stitch at all, since the threads are simply sewn down with small overcasting stitches. This is called couching and is a very important technique in appliqué work and free embroidery. The method can be used to fasten the patches on, to outline designs and also to cover whole surfaces. One advantage of this technique is that any kind of thread can be used, including those which could not be passed through the material.

The thread chosen for couching can be moved about until a suitable position is found for it, whether as a straight or curved line. And suddenly it seems much easier to draw in thread than in pencil. A pencil mark on a piece of paper must be rubbed out before it can be re-drawn but a piece of thread can be moved about until the correct position has been found, and then it can be sewn down. This is a great help to those of us who cannot draw very well!

It is usual to sew down with one thread of stranded cotton or sewing silk in a similar colour to the couched thread but you can use all sorts of other threads for freer work.

The overcasting stitches should normally be as invisible as possible. If, however, you want to emphasize them, you can always choose a colour which will contrast with the thread which is being sewn down.

A number of examples of couching can be seen in *fig. 61.* One of the most exciting aspects is the degree to which it is possible to modify the thread. It can be split, sewn on in irregular loops, coiled or twisted and then sewn on. It can be placed in neat little circles like miniature sailing-boat rigging.

The network is made up from thin threads, sewn on with very small sloping stitches, cross-stitches or four-sided stitches in a different colour. When you come to tighten the stitches in embroidery, it is often necessary to use a frame, otherwise pulling the threads might cause the material to pucker. Also it can be difficult to hold the laid threads in place unless the fabric is held taut. If you can pin the needlework to something, so that the threads are held taut in one direction, it is usually possible to manage very well. The threads should first be fastened in the centre, so that even long threads become manageable.

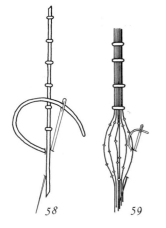

58   59

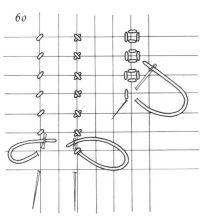

60

44

58. *Couching. The thread is sewn on with small overcast stitches.*

59. *The strands of a thread are separated and sewn on separately. Then are finally brought together again.*

60. *A network of threads can be fastened with small, slanting stitches, cross-stitches or four-sided stitches.*

61. *A surface with several varieties of couching – an exciting way of making patterns.*

61

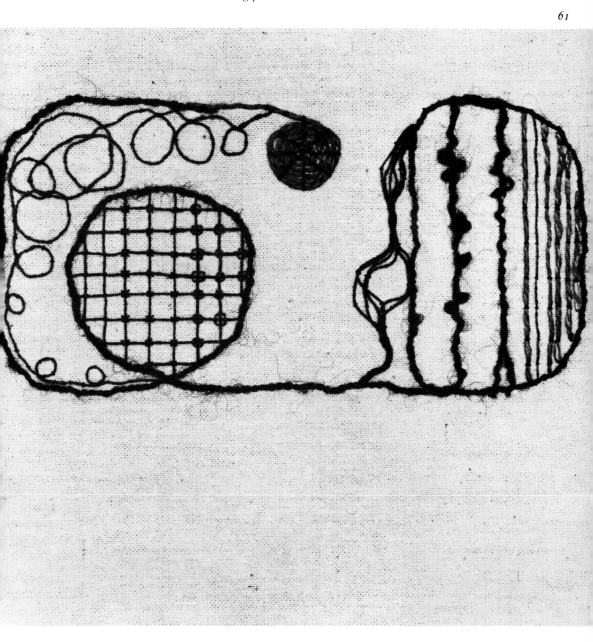

CHAIN STITCH

Like darning and couching, chain stitch is very suitable for long lines. A continuous line of chain stitches is always slightly wider and flatter than a couched line. This is why chain stitch is one of the most suitable for outlining, though it can be used in many other ways. The sketches below and the example in *fig. 70* show how chain stitch can be used and varied.

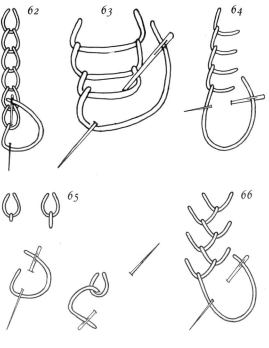

62. The usual chain stitch.

63. Open or square chain stitch.

64. Single feather stitch.

65. Detached chain stitches.

66. Feather stitches.

67. Twisted chain stitch.

68. Fly stitches embroidered next to each other sideways.

69. Fly stitches embroidered one within the other.

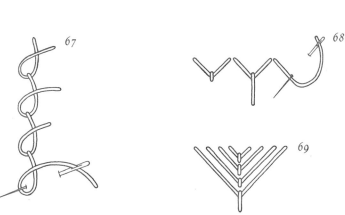

46

70. *A fantasy in chain stitches. All the stitches, although they look very different from each other, are derived from the ordinary chain stitch. This embroidered surface suggests plant cells or snail shells, or other natural forms.*

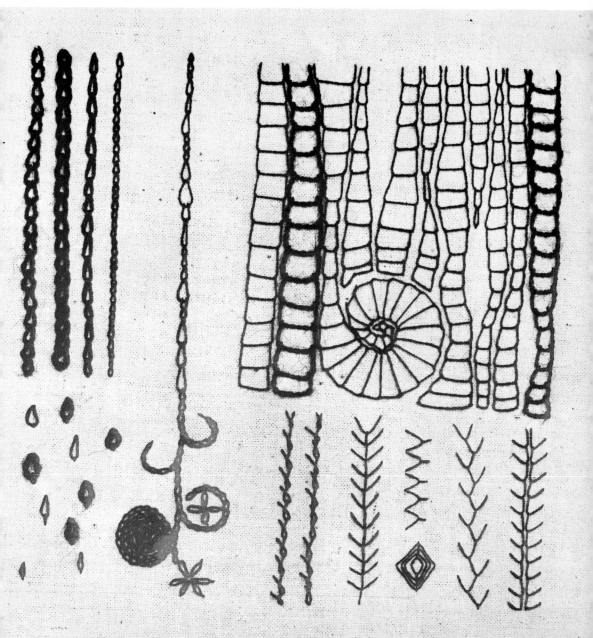

FOUR-SIDED STITCH

Four-sided stitches are often used in pulled or drawn fabric work and many readers will therefore already be acquainted with them. You can embroider long rows with them especially when the material is loosely woven. A very good way of covering a surface is to embroider them in rows but with a space left between each stitch.

When the material you are using is closely woven so that the threads cannot be counted easily, you have to work rather by eye and the stitches will not be so regular – they can even become triangular or pentagonal! You are not obliged to keep to horizontal and vertical lines, they can be embroidered in all directions. The technique may take some getting used to, but it is very satisfying to use this stitch in free embroidery.

When four-sided stitches are embroidered in rows, one below the other, they tend to look very much like open or square chain stitches making the transition from one to the other a logical progression. They do complement each other very well.

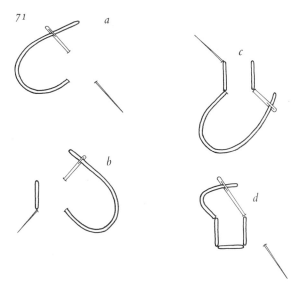

71. a, b, c, d. Four steps in making a four-sided stitch.

72. *Four-sided stitch and more four-sided stitches, set neatly next to each other, underneath each other, in a heap as if swept together, or in stripes and arcs, so that the final result is like a plan of New York.*

FRENCH KNOTS AND BULLION KNOTS

73

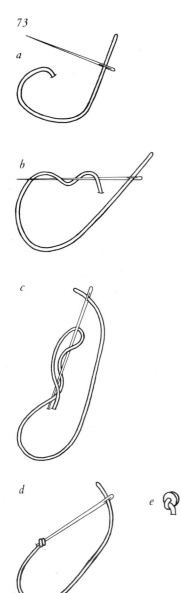

a

b

c

d

e

Knot stitches in embroidery are more than just putting the dots on the i's. If they are embroidered in thread of the same colour as the background material, they provide textural relief. This effect is heightened if different kinds of thread are used – thick and thin, rough and smooth. The sheen of the thread is exploited most fully when the knots are worked close together. With a smooth, silky thread, the knots become even brighter, and the effect is further emphasised if the background is of a dull material.

Working knots is admittedly not a speedy process, and the stitches also have the disadvantage that they cannot easily be unpicked. If you make a mistake, the best thing is to cut the thread on the reverse side of the work, between the knots, then pull the knots off from the front. These stitches, however, are still used for a great variety of work (see, for instance, *fig. 75* and many other illustrations in this book).

74

a

b

c

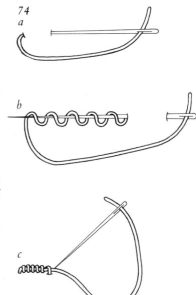

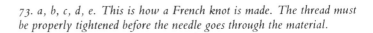

73. a, b, c, d, e. *This is how a French knot is made. The thread must be properly tightened before the needle goes through the material.*

74. a, b, c. *This is the way to make bullion knots.*

50

75. French knots and bullion knots in the same colour as the background material give a pleasant relief effect. Coloured beads can be added. The knots on the left have not been tightened properly. This effect can be fun, but the loops must be fastened tightly here and there.

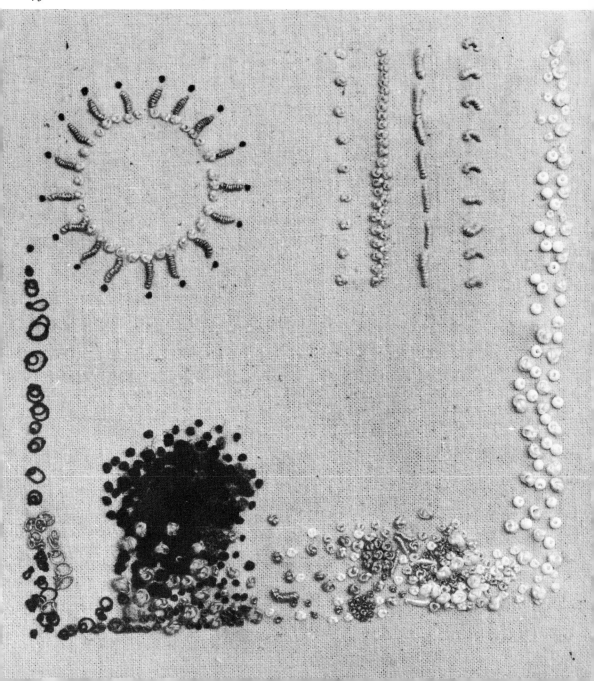

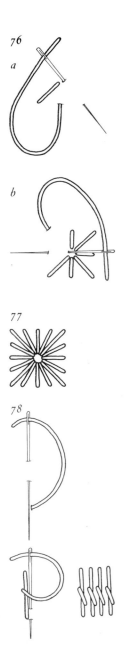

It is customary to use star stitches or eye stitches in counted thread embroidery such as pulled or drawn fabric work. But what is there to prevent us from using these stitches in different ways? They can be neat and regular or completely irregular, with any number of radii.

If they are to be embroidered on tightly-woven material, as in *fig. 80*, you should use a thin thread, such as one or two strands of stranded cotton, otherwise the work would become too coarse. A relief effect is produced if the stitches are embroidered with a bead in the centre.

Two other stitches are shown in *fig. 80*: Roumanian stitch and Vandyke stitch. They can be embroidered in wide or narrow bands, either with stitches very close together or slightly apart, using a dull or a shiny thread. In this way they create a very lively background.

Vandyke stitch forms a band with a central ridge and long or short extensions on either side. The relief effect is very apparent, due to the play of the shadows thrown by the stitches. The rougher threads, such as wool and linen, give the best result and create the most shadow.

Roumanian stitch is much flatter than Vandyke stitch. If the stitches are embroidered far apart, they become spikey and disconnected. You can achieve a heavy or light effect, according to how you vary the spacing between the stitches.

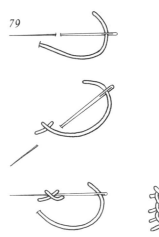

76. a. b. *The star stitch is embroidered with each stitch taken down in the centre from the outside, so that the central hole remains open. More rays can be added if required.*

77. *Star stitch with sixteen stitches embroidered in a square.*

78. *Roumanian stitch.*

79. *Vandyke stitch makes a very definite relief, rather like a ridge in sand.*

80. *Regular and irregular star stitches. These stitches can be even more varied on loosely woven material. The relief effect can be even further accentuated when the stitch is decorated with a bead. The bands on the right are made with Roumanian stitch and Vandyke stitch.*

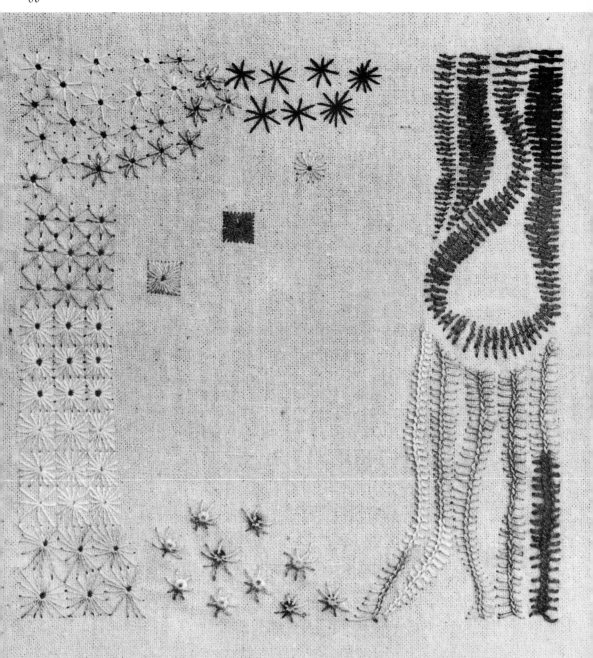

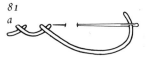

LACE STITCHES

This technique is great fun, because the stitches form a kind of netting on the background material. This netting can be thick and knotty – for instance, if you use pearl cotton and sew the stitches very close together. A light and airy effect can be achieved by using a thin thread and large stitches. If you want to do this, it is often advisable to fix the netting here and there to the background material with small stitches, otherwise the long loops may get entangled.

The examples of lace stitches on the right, in *fig. 84*, are very similar to Vandyke stitches. Although they are slightly wider, the method is the same. When the stitches have to cover a wide area, the thread can become too long on the reverse side of the material, as you always have to go back to the same side to begin. If this is the case, it may be advisable to fasten off after each row.

The other lace stitches are embroidered in rows from side to side, the needle is only passed through the material at the end of every row. Each loop can have one or more loops worked into it or some can be passed over. Different threads can be introduced depending on the effect desired.

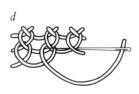

As illustrated in *fig. 84*, lace stitches are ideal for making a piece of netting over a space cut in the material. Since you can see what is behind the embroidery through the mesh, you will understand why the background plays such an important role in the final composition. A new dimension is added to an otherwise flat piece of embroidery.

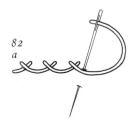

83

81. *The working method for these lace stitches is the same as for Vandyke stitch – but with more stitches next to one another.*

82. *Lace stitches embroidered from side to side in rows.*

83. *One or more stitches can be made in each loop, while other loops can be missed altogether.*

84. Lace stitches lie as a kind of net on the material and frequently give it an exciting texture. Lace stitches can also be used to decorate holes or spaces in the background material.

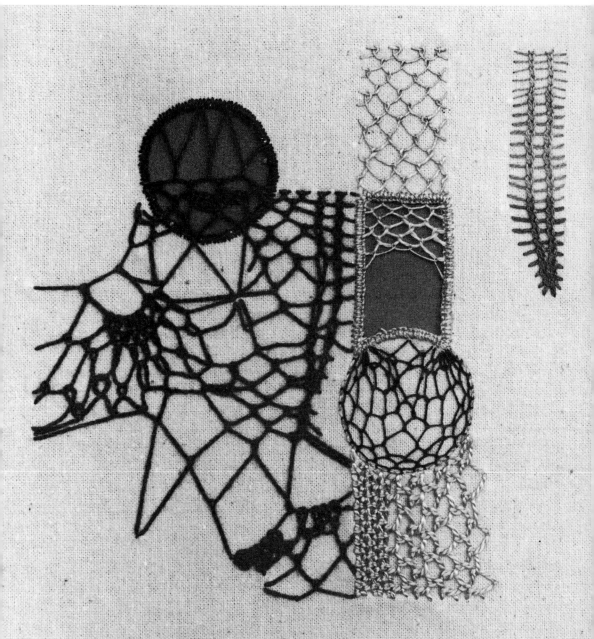

WOVEN PICOTS, WORKED LOOPS AND LONG STRAIGHT STITCHES

One of the most exciting exercises in embroidery is to build up raised areas on the surface.

This effect can be achieved by using woven picots, buttonholed or whipped loops, French and bullion knots, beads, and long straight stitches. The straight stitches are gathered up here and there with small overcast stitches, taking care that the stretched threads do not become too long near the outer edge of the work.

It is necessary to use an embroidery frame when doing stitches which span long distances.

85

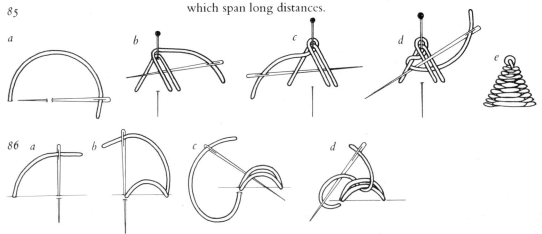

86

87

85. *Picots and beads embroidered together. A pin is used to hold taut the thread which defines the picot.*

86. *Loops made with button-hole stitches.*

87. *On the left, picots are used to bring strong relief effect to the surface of the material. If this is continued into the borders it can give an unusual finishing touch (see page 84, colour).*

88. *Picots do not have to be embroidered only along the border, they can look very good anywhere in the work. This is also true for the loops, even if it does make them look a bit untidy. The loops are held bunched together by overcast stitches.*

CHANGING PATTERNED FABRICS WITH EMBROIDERY STITCHES

89. Small stripes can be embroidered in such a way that lighter and darker areas appear on the material.

90. Wide, straight stripes can be broken up with the aid of embroidery.

In the chapter on embroidered surfaces we have seen how to add patterns and textures to a plain background. But materials which are already patterned can also be changed – the pattern accentuated or softened, or even changed completely. With this kind of work, it is absolutely essential to aim for harmony between the background pattern and the embroidery.

STRIPES

In the case of striped material, light-coloured stripes can be made to disappear by embroidering over them with yarn of the same colour as the darker stripes (fig. 89).

An undulating effect can be given to straight stripes by running the colour of one stripe into the colour of the stripe next to it. They can interlock with one another and in this way a plain striped material can become full of life and interest (fig. 90).

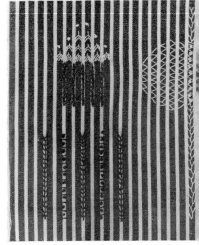

89

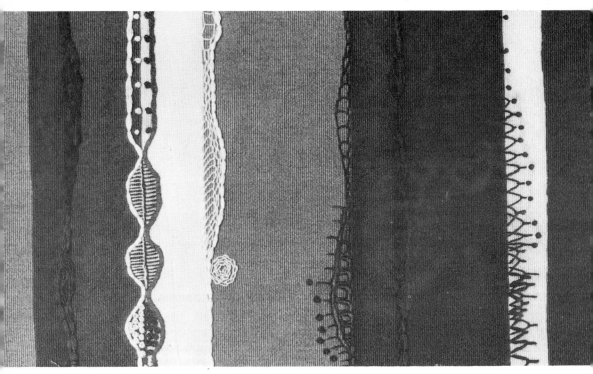

90

91. *If the black and white checks are made larger, the effect will be completely different from that of the original pattern.*

92. *Spots can be strung together or combined to make lighter areas. Or they can be made to disappear or become square checks.*

CHECKS AND SPOTS

The patterns on check materials are often almost too regular and too rectangular to be used with other patches. They can, however, be modified if necessary.

A dark check can be made larger by embroidering one or more rows of four-sided stitches around it, or smaller by embroidering a four-sided stitch in lighter colour along the edge of the check itself.

A dark check can be made to disappear if you embroider on it with light-coloured thread. You can use four-sided stitches, knot stitches, cross stitches and chain stitches, depending on the size of the check. Although it may strike us as a bit stiff and old-fashioned, this technique can be a lot of fun and can form the basis of a free approach. The checks in *fig. 91* no longer look straight and square, but rather like an enlargement of the screen of a newspaper photograph.

Spots can also be made bigger or smaller. They can be turned into bead chains on a string or be made to form completely new patterns.

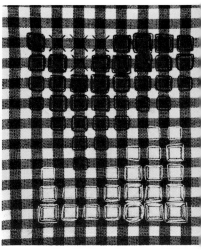

91

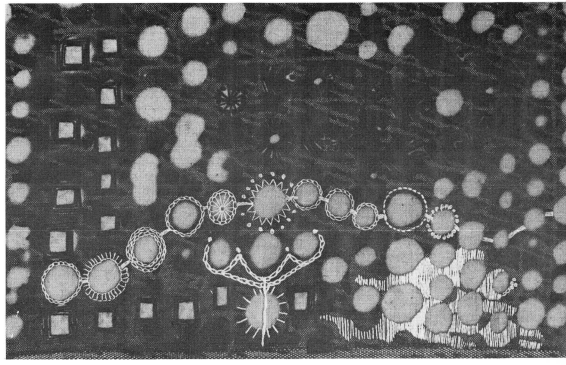

92

AIDS TO DESIGNING

PAPER MOSAIC

Many people are intimidated by the thought of working out a design and embroidering it – it often seems so difficult and complicated. In this chapter, I want to discuss a number of aids which will help you to create simple designs.

Paper is a very important help, either newspaper, colourful pages out of women's magazines, coloured transparent tissue-paper, wrapping paper or wallpaper, all of which can be used for mosaics and cuttings.

If you tear a particular shape out of a piece of paper, the edges will be left rather frayed and irregular. They are never as neat as you expect, but this gives the shapes a particular charm.

You can either use whole, large pieces of paper for a paper mosaic, or you can compose shapes out of several little pieces.

Next, the pieces of paper should be stuck down on a sheet of drawing paper. If you are using coloured transparent tissue paper for the mosaic, even more subtle effects can be created by making the pieces overlap partially or completely. First, you can try making a house, a tree, a fish, a sun or some other simple shape. It is also fun to arrange the shapes on the drawing paper so that they form a balanced composition. You will soon discover that it is easier to work with large shapes. Very small or jagged cuttings are difficult to handle, and you will find that exactly the same applies when you come to work with material.

Tearing paper and sticking it down in this way is very helpful – it means that people who cannot draw well can really let themselves go and come up with something personal. It also provides a link between the original inspiration and the finished work, helping to develop a feeling for shape and the way in which a composition can be put together.

93. A shape can be torn out of paper in one piece. . . .

94. . . . or it can be made up of many small pieces.

95. Arbitrarily chosen shapes become an abstract composition.

93

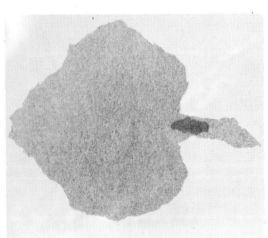

94

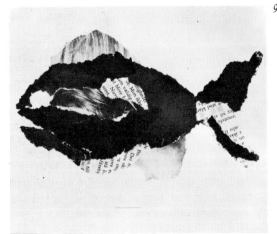

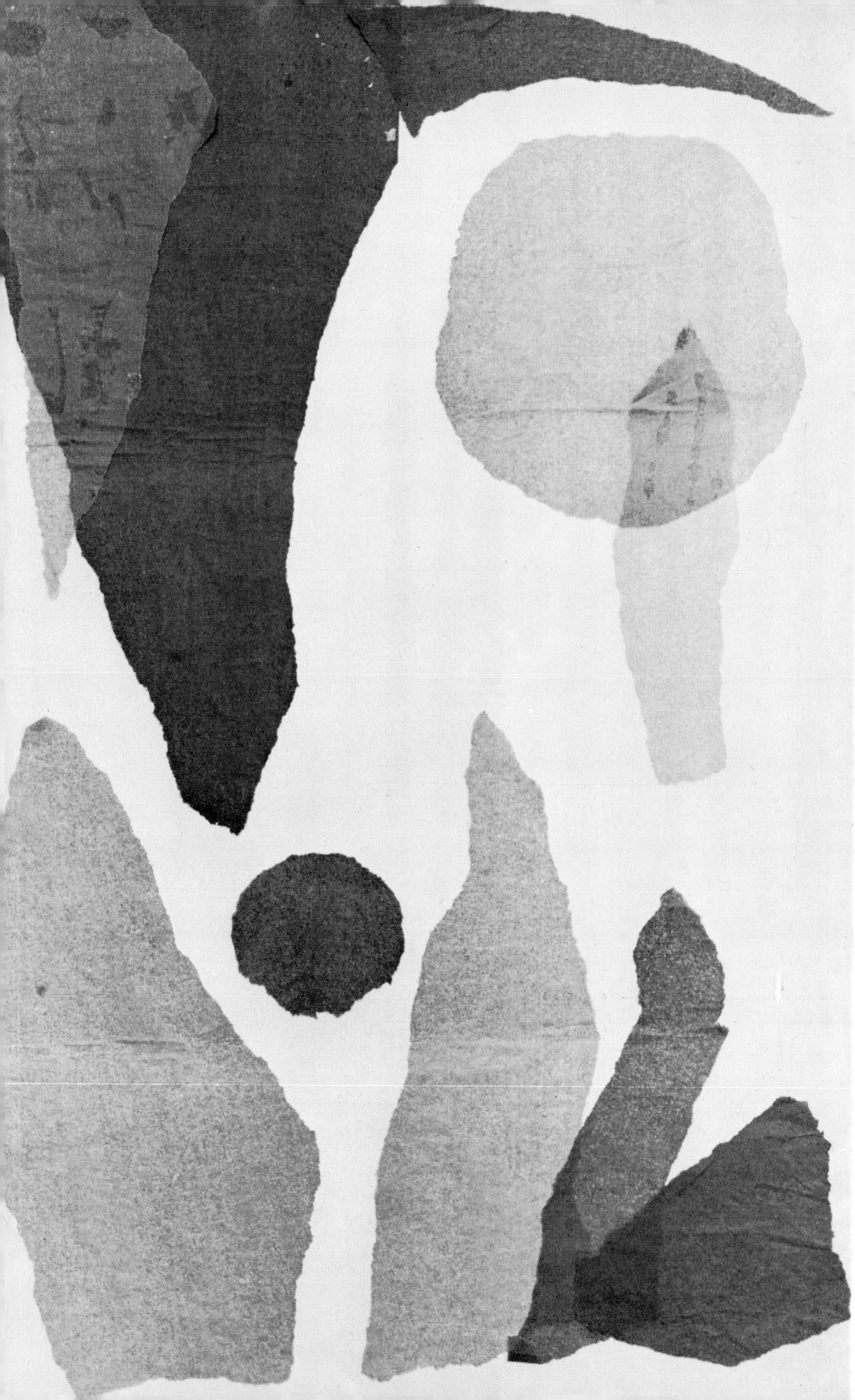

96

96. *Very little is needed to make a composition to work from (see page 84, colour).*

97. *Tearing and sticking paper down is a good way of discovering subjects. Apples and other fruits are good subjects for paper mosaics and, later, appliqué work (see page 85, colour).*

If you use newspaper or paper from a women's magazine, you can also make use of the pattern created by the print. This is a good exercise for helping you to discover and use the ideas suggested by various patterns. You can choose a particular picture or section of text, keeping in mind the role it has to play in your mosaic. This will help you to learn how to look for the right materials and which pieces to cut out. Your final composition does not have to look like anything specific, as long as it is harmonious.

98

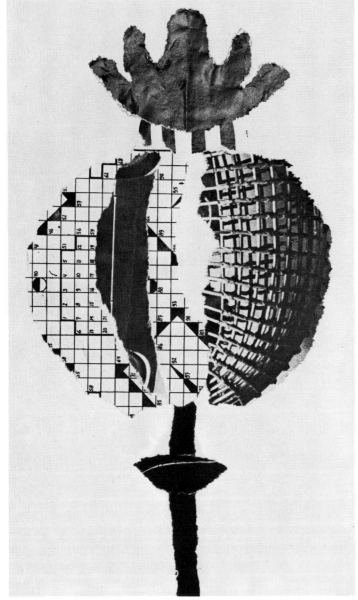

98. The pattern and colour of the paper as well as the shape of the torn-out pieces also play a part in the composition. Here is a mosaic of the dry seed-box of a poppy.

99. The influence of the paper mosaic is clearly visible in the materials chosen (see page 86, colour).

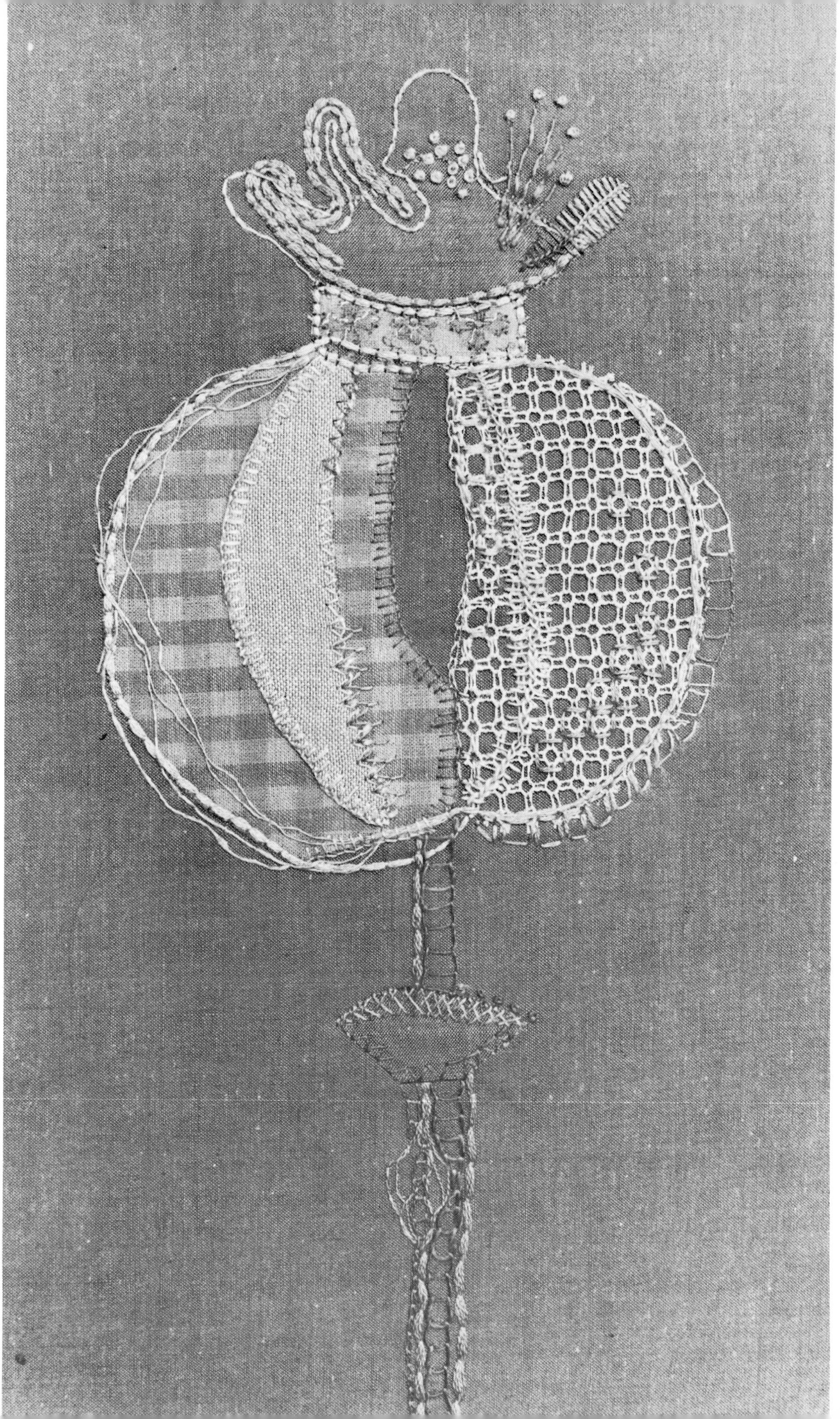

Paper can also be used for making patterns by cutting. The shapes used in torn mosaics are more or less formed by chance. If you cut the paper however, the shapes will be more precise – even if you are a beginner and a little awkward, this does not matter.

There are many possibilities. You can, for example, cut out geometrical shapes and use these in a composition. You can cut out one large piece and cut it up into smaller pieces. If you reassemble all these pieces again, like a jigsaw, you will get back to the original shape. But if you reassemble the pieces slightly askew and make them overlap here and there, it will no longer be possible to cover the background completely. There will be gaps in the paper and the outline will be irregular, making a much more interesting shape than the original *(see fig. 101)*.

CUTTINGS

100. A house can be made from the geometrical figures printed on wall-paper.

101. Cuttings with spaces between them. A large leaf-shape has been divided into smaller pieces and then put together again slightly askew. The gaps between the pieces give the effect of veins on the leaf (see page 85, colour).

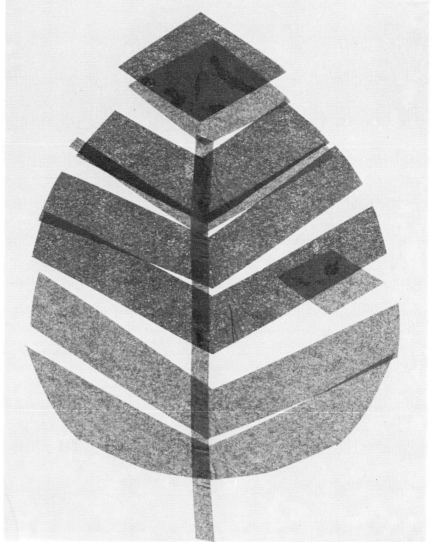

101

PAPER STRIPS

If you fold a piece of paper several times, you can make a whole row of similar shapes by cutting through all the layers of paper at once. The shapes will hang together, meeting at the folds. In this way, you can make a row of birds or fish, or a circle of dancing girls.

Notice, too, how the strip of paper looks when the shapes have been cut out. Perhaps you will learn something unexpected from it! The strip which is left over has just as much potential as the shapes which have been cut out, for decorating borders or making complete compositions.

102. A very simple bird border. . . .

103. . . . and the cutting left over when the birds have been cut out.

104, 105. New borders have been made with the left-over cuttings. The shapes are very simple and very enjoyable to work with.

106. Imaginary trees – the result of creative work with scissors.

107. The cuttings still have a surprise in store for us – more imaginary trees.

108. Fish in a row.

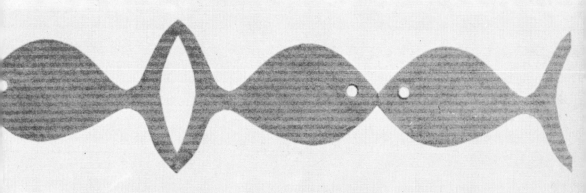

109. Doodling.

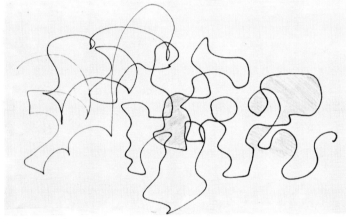

110. A simple game.

DOODLES

Some people find chance effects the most helpful. Try doodling with a pencil on a piece of paper and see if a shape develops which could be used in a composition. Anyone can doodle on a piece of paper, then it is only a question of recognising what could be useful. Just try it once! Even if nothing comes of it, you will at least have spent a few hours in relaxation, letting the pencil find its own way on the paper. It doesn't have to be taken too seriously – it is only an aid to making better compositions.

112. Doodling will sometimes suggest an idea. In this shape, there are suggestions for applied patches, holes in the material and also embroidered surfaces.

111. Using a pencil.

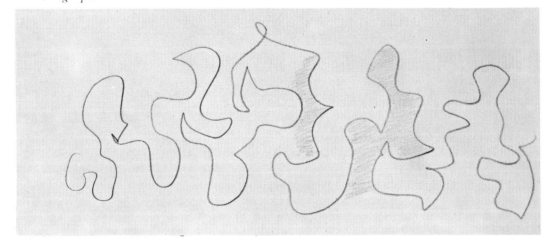

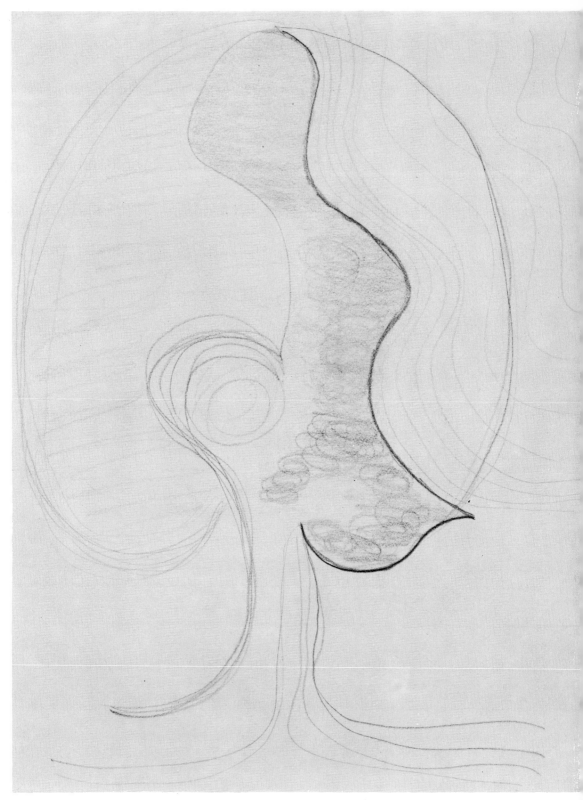

A THREAD

A thread which is simply dropped on to a piece of material can also be the starting-point for a design.

This is a particularly exciting way of beginning a composition, because you are not working towards a specific end; you see what happens, using the ideas which suggest themselves as you go along.

The thread can be sewn on to the material in the curves and twists which have been created accidentally when it was dropped on to the fabric. Some of the areas formed on the material in this way can have patches applied to them, others can be filled up with stitching or couching. Other areas can be cut out and the spaces filled with lace stitches. Give free rein to your imagination!

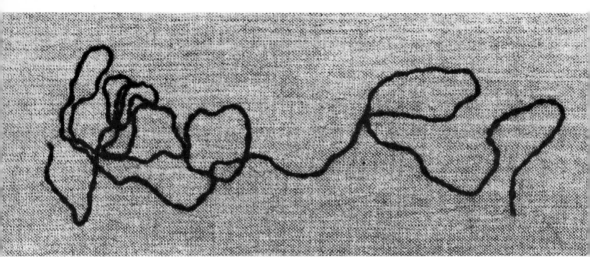

113

114

72

The small wall hanging in *fig. 115* had precisely such a beginning. A woollen thread dropped on a small patch of material made a flower shape and this provided the starting-point; that is why the leaves were given a texture which suggests a plant's cells and veins. The flower itself became so large that it started to hang. The material in the area below right has been repeated as edging along the top, and this has been carried on around the outline of the appliqué. On the far left an orange oval on a long stalk has grown into a delicate flower. Along the stalk, several woven picots have been made green like the stalk, while the rest have been made purple-red, like the edging on the right. All these small details, the repetition of motifs and the constant play of thread and colour make this embroidery technique very exciting.

113. A thread is dropped on a piece of material and gives the imagination something to work on.

114. Here is the result. A journey into the unknown. Are those mountains and a cactus, or something quite different?

115. The starting-point was a game with a piece of thread, which turned itself into a flowershape. The areas defined by the thread can be treated in different ways.

DRAWING

Drawings provide a good basis for a composition with fabric and thread. Even rudimentary sketches can be useful; it is the basic shapes which matter, not the detail of a finished drawing. The simpler the sketch, the easier it is to work on.

You can look for your inspiration in advertisements, posters or even children's drawings. All these things use basically simple shapes, so they provide ideal starting-points for design in appliqué work. Make sure you always have a pencil ready to take down any design which you may be able to use later.

116. Peacock. In this pattern, only a few areas are defined, but they suggest enough possibilities for further development.

117. A simple drawing is advisable.

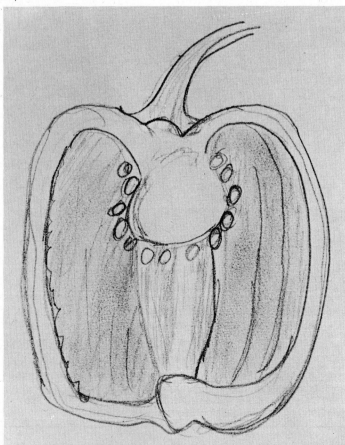

118. And this is how a cut pepper looks in appliqué.

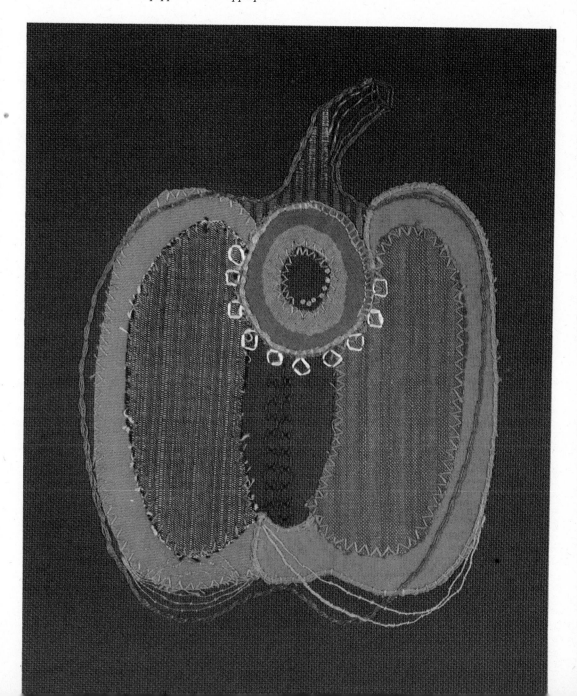

119. *Every shape and drawing can be used in innumerable ways. When shapes are put next to each other, they sometimes look very different.*

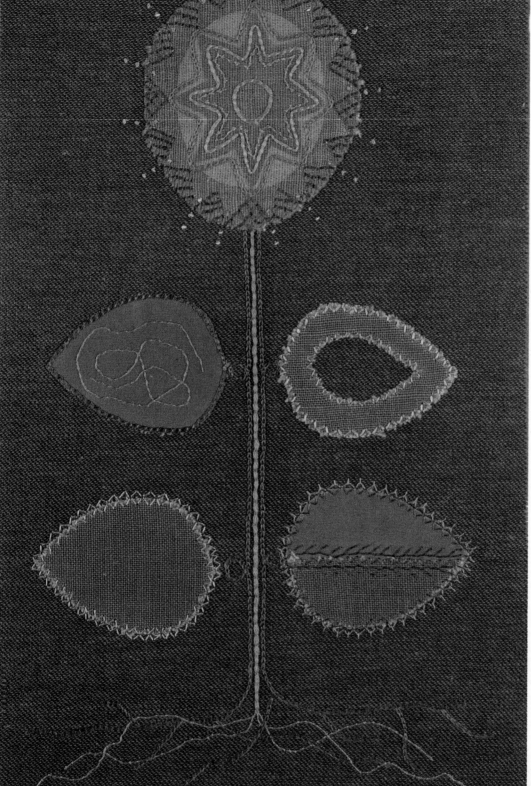

STARTING FROM THE MATERIAL

The material itself can also be a considerable help in putting together a composition or designing a pattern. And this applies equally to smaller patches of material which are to be sewn on, and to the larger pieces which will be used as the background for a whole composition. The pattern can either be emphasised in parts by embroidery, or covered by patches, according to your personal taste. Material with a rather hazy pattern – hand-printed fabrics, for instance – is most likely to stimulate the imagination. This kind of fabric is better suited to be the background in a wall-hanging than a plain one. You should not, however, underestimate the difficulty of using the pattern of the material as the starting-point for your own design. The problem is to combine this pattern harmoniously with the one which you have in your own mind.

121

122

120. *The printed star in the oval flower looks better for being emphasized with embroidery.*

121. *Have you seen my pretty embroidered nose?*

122. *I'm going now. That was all.*

27

30

39

96

93

87

84

FINISHING OFF

Although I am not going to discuss this stage at length, many people are alarmed by it, so let me give you a few examples in which the finishing off is only the continuation of the embroidery and just as much fun as the embroidery itself.

HEMMING THE BACKGROUND MATERIAL

For hemming, the background material should not be too thick. The reverse side of the material should either be the same as the upper side or be of such a colour and texture that it forms an attractive hem when it is folded to the right side.

The turnings are folded towards the right side and sewn down with a couching stitch or a row of darning stitches. See the work method in figs. 124–7.

This method of finishing off is suitable for all small bell-pulls, braids, table runners; also for the hems of aprons, children's skirts and all items which do not need lining.

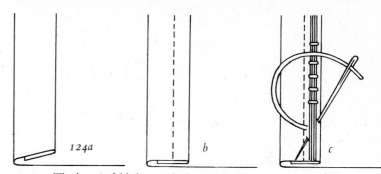

124a   b   c

124. a. The hem is folded towards the right side.
b. The hem is tacked into place.
c. A thread is sewn along the edge. The overcast stitches must go through the three layers of material.

125. The hem can also be sewn with wave stitches.

126. The border is further decorated with fly stitches and french knots.

127. With small hems, the edges can be treated like this. To hang the article up, a rod can be passed through the hem.

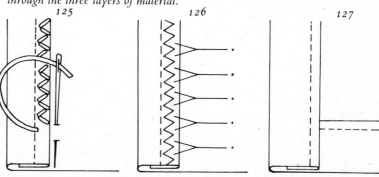

125   126   127

HEMMING WITH A DIFFERENT MATERIAL

Some needlework requires a framed effect. This can be achieved with a number of fabrics of different colours or with a plain material. A colour which has been used in the main composition can be continued in the hem to produce a very pleasant effect (see *fig. 87, page 84*). First, you fold the edges of your work underneath and tack them to the reverse side. This should give you a very good idea of what still has to be done to finish it off. The background surrounding the main motif can, of course, be made up of several parts and *figs. 128* and *129* show how these pieces can be tacked round on to the reverse side of a wall hanging. When the edge of the framing material or materials has been tacked (basted) to the reverse side, it can be secured on the right side in the following ways:

with the machine,
with small, invisible stitches,
with couching,
with wave stitch,
or with a row of French knots. You should see that you go through all the layers of material to make sure that the hem is properly sewn. Alternatively, you can finish off with woven picots (*page 56*), buttonholed loops (*page 56*), or a fringe with beads (see *fig. 130*). When the hemming is completed the whole article should be lined with a thin piece of material. The lining at the lower edge of the article should be left loose. In the case of larger articles, it is advisable to insert a woven interlining between the material and the lighter lining.

128. Two strips of material form the border; they are sewn on to the reverse side of the work then turned over the edges and fastened into place on the upper side.

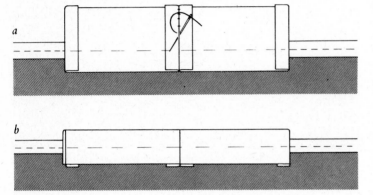

129. This is how a corner is made in a protruding border.

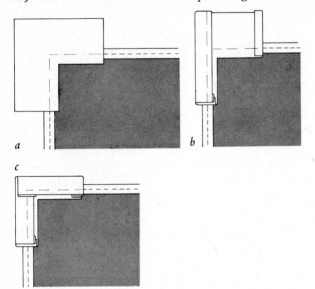

130. If the composition looks rather stiff, you can always make a fancy border.

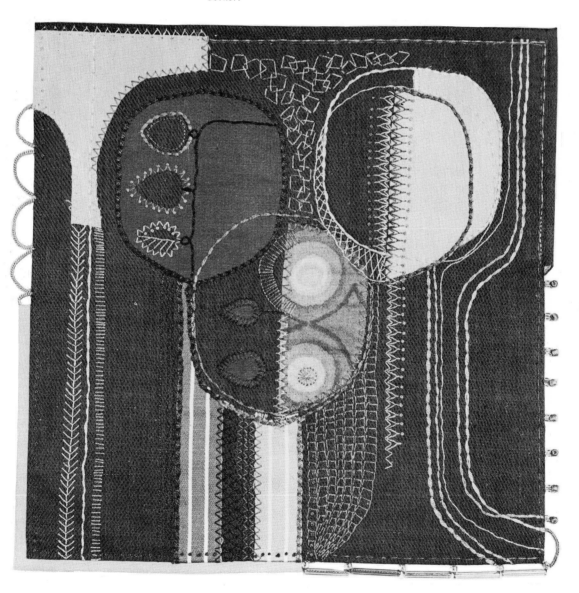

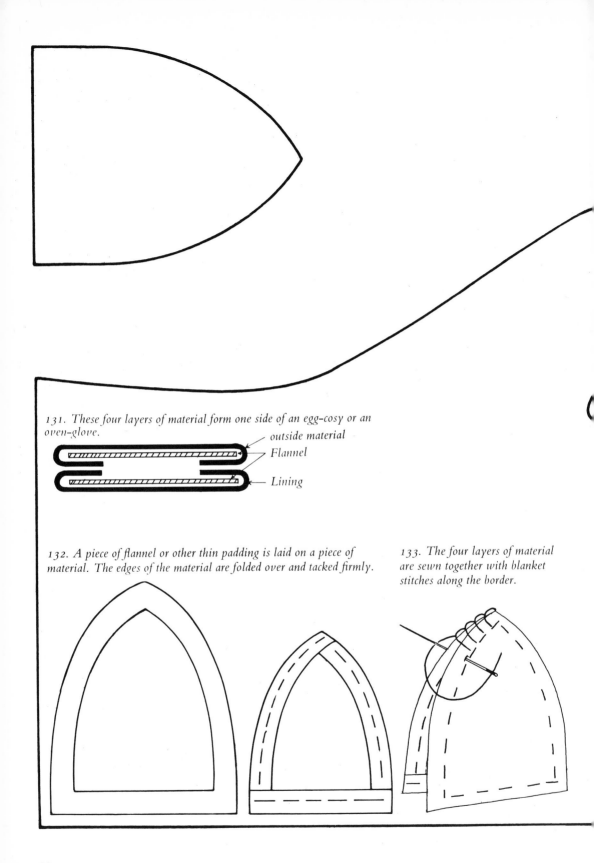

131. These four layers of material form one side of an egg-cosy or an oven-glove.

outside material

Flannel

Lining

132. A piece of flannel or other thin padding is laid on a piece of material. The edges of the material are folded over and tacked firmly.

133. The four layers of material are sewn together with blanket stitches along the border.

EGG-COSIES AND OVEN-GLOVES

The finishing off of smaller items, such as egg-cosies and oven-gloves, can be quite difficult, because the inner lining is often so thick that it makes a very unsightly hem. The following method is not particularly quick, but the result is pleasing to look at.

The egg-cosy is triangular (*fig. 135*). Each of the three sides is

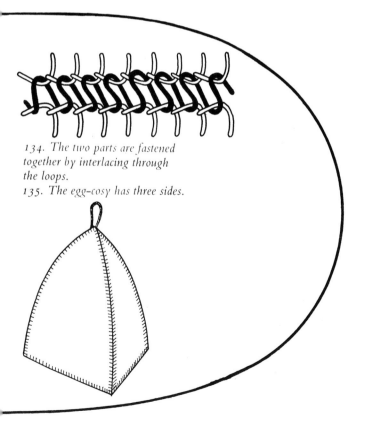

134. *The two parts are fastened together by interlacing through the loops.*

135. *The egg-cosy has three sides.*

composed of a layer of material on the outside, then two layers of flannel, domestic or other thin padding material, and another lining layer. The pieces of flannel are cut according to the pattern, but with no extra allowance for hems, whereas the material for the outside and the inner lining are cut with this allowance. A flannel triangle is placed on one of the outer triangles. The border to be hemmed is folded back on to the flannel and tacked down (see *fig. 132*). In the same way, a piece of the lining material is tacked on to the second piece of flannel. The two parts are sewn together with blanket stitches along the edge so that the needle passes through the two layers of flannel, which are then sufficiently well held in place for the cosy to be washed. When the three parts have been embroidered with blanket stitches, they are assembled two by two by interlacing a thread through the loops from one side to the other (*fig. 134*).

The oven-glove is made in exactly the same way. For each glove you need: two layers of material for the outside and two layers of lining material (all four should be cut with an extra allowance for the hems) and four layers of flannel or other suitable padding material (without turnings). The outer layer and the inner layers are prepared separately and then finally put together by passing a thread through the loops of the border stitching (*fig. 134*).

CHOOSING THE COLOURS

One of the difficulties – and one of the charms – of designing your own embroidery and appliqué work lies in the choice of coloured patches and coloured threads.

The choice of colours depends very much on the mood and temperament of the person who is doing the embroidery. For some people, the process is quite easy: they choose colours which harmonise and combine pleasantly, without being really conscious of how they made their choice. Other people find if diffcult and, having weighed all the pros and cons carefully, still fail to produce something pleasing. This is why I have decided to give some directions on the choice of colours.

There are, of course, thousands of shades and colours and it seems an impossible task to bring some semblance of order to them. But only when this has been done, will we be able to understand and use colour.

Many people – both artists and scientists – have devoted themselves to this problem in the past and have drawn up a number of two-dimensional and three-dimensional colour systems. I do not intend to go into these systems in detail, as there are specialist books on the subject.

Here, then, is a very simple method of classifying colours and a few directions for those who find choosing them a difficult business.

CLASSIFICATION

If you take a number of reddish-coloured threads, you can try to sort them into groups or rows which will show a gradual colour progression.

You will see that some of the threads are bright, others dark, and some relatively pale. These are differences in the degree of intensity or tone value of the colour.

Then, you can group the threads into yellowish reds (orange-reds) and bluish reds. These are variations of hue.

Yellow, red and blue hold a special place among basic colours. They are called primary colours (fig. 136). All other colours can be obtained by mixing these primary colours. Lighter colours can be made by adding white to a colour (or by thinning). Dark colours are made by adding black to a colour. Black itself is a mixture of equal parts of the three primary colours. You obtain green by mixing yellow and blue, violet by mixing red and blue, and orange by mixing red and yellow.

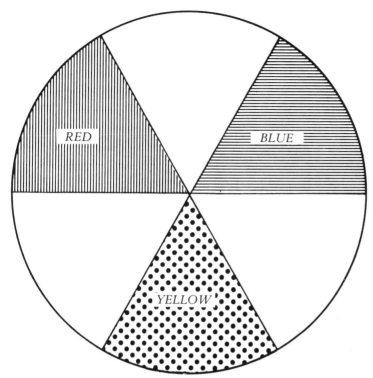

136. *Colour circle with three primary colours.*

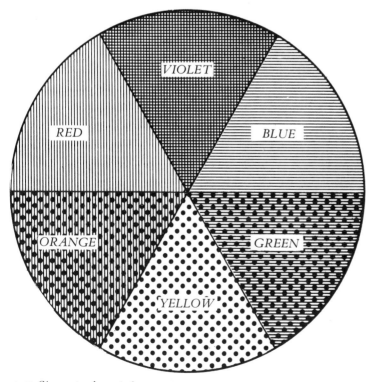

137. *Six-part colour circle.*

THE COLOUR CIRCLE

The six colours can be arranged in a circle (*fig. 137*), so that it is possible to progress from one colour to another: red – orange – yellow – green – blue – violet. Any two colours which lie opposite each other in the circle are called complementary colours. Thus there are here three sets of complementary colours: yellow – violet, red – green, orange – blue.

THE TWELVE-PART COLOUR CIRCLE

If the colour circle is further divided by blending two colours which lie next to each other, you get a circle divided as in *fig. 138*, in which there are twelve different colour tones. Continuing in this fashion, the circle can be divided into any number of sectors.

The series of colour tones in such a circle is composed of colours which have been obtained by mixing two primary colours. However, a lot of colours are excluded from the circle; for example, those which are obtained by mixing three primary colours. A more complicated system has to be devised to take account of them but a thorough examination of the subject would occupy more space than we have here; it is sufficient for you to know that these colours exist.

This colour circle demonstrates that:

a. the closer two colours lie to each other, the closer they are related to each other;

b. the further apart they are, the greater the difference between them;

c. when two colours lie opposite each other, the difference is greatest, being a complete contrast. These colours are called contrasting or complementary.

93

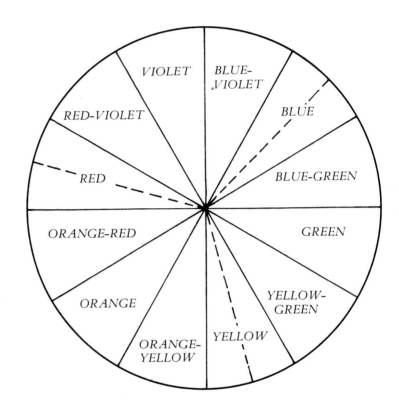

138. *Twelve-part colour circle.*

COLOUR HARMONY

If we take the twelve-part colour circle as our starting-point, it will be possible to establish a method for choosing matching colours. Choose, for instance:

1. one colour in different degrees of intensity or tone value – that is, a progression from light to dark in the same colour. This produces a sober and refined harmony.
Example: light yellow – yellow – dark yellow.
2. a colour from two neighbouring sectors of the colour circle. A nice restful harmony.
Example: orange-red – red.
3. colours from three neighbouring sectors of the colour circle. Still a pleasant, rather unobtrusive harmony.
Example: yellow – yellow-green – green.

4. colours from one quarter of the circle. There is an element of freshness in the harmony.

Example: yellow – yellow-green – green – blue-green.

5. colours from a third of the colour circle, bordered by two primary colours. There is now tension in the harmony.

Example: red – red-violet – violet – blue-violet – blue.

6. colours from a third of the colour circle, but now on both sides of a primary colour. This produces a harmony with a lot of tension. Very difficult for the inexperienced.

Example: orange-red – red – red-violet – violet – blue-violet *(fig. 87, page 84,* shows an example from this category).

If colours from more than five sectors are chosen the harmony will no longer hold together; there are too many colours and the composition looks far too restless.

CONTRAST

To strengthen a colour harmony, a complementary colour can be introduced to bring a note of contrast. This is frequently done in painting.

There are a number of examples of the use of contrasting colours in this book:

fig. 115, page 73: the colours chosen are orange-red – red – red-violet – violet, with yellow-green as a contrast.

fig. 118, page 75 shows the harmonizing colours of: yellow – yellow-green – green, with a violet as a contrast.

fig. 46, page 83: the colours are blue – blue-green – green, with red as a contrast.

DISCORDANT COLOURS

A combination of colours can be discordant, as well as harmonious. Such a combination shocks the eye, but can be very effective for drawing attention to something; it can even make a very harmonious composition more interesting. This clash of colour will usually occur when a colour is drawn from a different sector in the circle from the other colours, and is much lighter, much darker or much brighter than the other colours.

These are a few suggestions as to why some colour combinations are more successful than others, but no guide should prevent the you from going your own way and trying out other combinations. You can find your inspiration anywhere – in paintings, in shop windows and especially in nature, which is surely the best teacher. You can learn something from everything you see. How much you learn depends on how much you are prepared to experiment with colours and their combination.

INSPIRATION

The most extraordinary circumstances can be sources of inspiration. The principle is that you should look carefully and let what you see work on your imagination.

Broken window panes become a composition of dark and light rectangles.

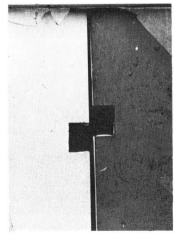

Old houses due for demolition or the facades along a street can also suggest designs.

A strange interplay of lines is created when caterpillars make their cocoons among the plants. . . .

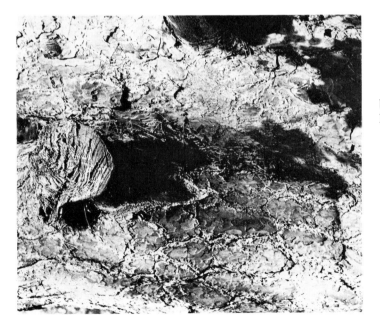

. . . and a sawn-off bough becomes imperceptibly a moon landscape.

Even gnarled wood or a weathered wall can give new impetus to the imagination.

Varied surfaces and lines compete with each other to make the biggest impression on the retentive mind. Can we be quick enough to capture the fleeting impression?

FURTHER STITCHERY BOOKS FROM VAN NOSTRAND REINHOLD

INDEX